BUILDANEWLIFE

BY CREATING YOUR DREAM HOME

First published in Great Britain in 2007 by
Cassell Illustrated, a division of Octopus Publishing Group Limited
2–4 Heron Quays, London E14 4JP

Text by George Clarke with Samantha Scott-Jeffries

Editorial, design and layout by
Essential Works, 168a Camden Street, London NW1 9PT
www.essentialworks.co.uk
Project Manager: Fiona Screen
Designer: Barbara Doherty
Proofreader: Barbara Dixon
Indexer: Hazel Bell

All photographs courtesy of Shine Limited
except pages 97–8, 160–171 courtesy of George Clarke

A CIP catalogue record for this book is available from the British Library.

ISBN-13: 978-1-84403568-7
ISBN-10: 1-84403-568-9

The author and publisher cannot accept liability for any loss, damage, or
injury incurred as a result (directly or indirectly) of the advice and
information contained in this book or in the use or application of the
contents of this book.

The information in this book is intended as a guide only; anyone
contemplating buying property as an investment, and/ or making alterations
to their property, should seek independent financial and other appropriate
professional advice.

BUILDANEWLIFE

BY CREATING YOUR DREAM HOME

GEORGE CLARKE

CASSELL ILLUSTRATED

CONTENTS

Introduction

There are two moments in my life I remember so clearly that it now seems obvious that I should have made a television series called *Build A New Life in the Country*.

The first was one of my earliest childhood memories. Both of my grandfathers were builders and I remember sitting in the cabin of an enormous JCB earthmover with my Granddad Dunbar and watching him tearing and pushing at the hard North-East landscape on a freezing cold winter's day to construct another building in Sunderland. I must have only been four or five years old. Most kids my age were content playing in their back gardens with toy diggers. But not me. I wanted the real thing. I would do anything to visit a building site. These days it wouldn't be allowed because of strict health and safety laws, but back then I could hang out on site for hours and hours pretending to be one of the building crew, digging my own little foundations, carrying bricks, nailing timber and having greasy fry-ups with sugary cups of tea in Portacabins packed with blokes covered in sweat, dust and mud. These guys were tough grafters, with hands like shovels, working unbelievably hard to put food on the table at home and help to build Britain … I loved it! Before long I began filling sketchbooks with scratchy pencil drawings of construction details and building façades. I didn't just want to construct buildings; I wanted to design them. At the tender age of 12 I decided I would become an architect.

The second moment was at the age of 16. I lived in a busy town in the North-East of England and I'd hardly ever ventured out into the English countryside. Then one day my Uncle Jonny, a keen fell-walker, asked if I'd like to join him on a day trip to the Lake District to climb the

> Go confidently in the direction of your dreams! Live the life you've imagined.
>
> Henry David Thoreau

beautiful fells on the west side of Derwentwater.

I couldn't believe that such a wonderful place could exist only two hours' drive away from Sunderland. Being able to venture out across miles of open landscape, amongst nature and wildlife, while breathing in the cleanest fresh air and relaxing in the peace and tranquillity of rural life I felt that I'd been transported to another world. It was a complete contrast to the grime and stresses of inner-city building sites and it was a day that changed my life forever.

In other words, being on building sites made me decide to become an architect and being in the countryside made me fall in love with our landscape and inspired me to renovate and build beautiful houses there.

The television series *Build a New Life in the Country*, and this book that accompanies it, illustrates all that I feel passionate about – people making their dreams come true by restoring some of the most wonderful old British buildings in the most beautiful parts of the countryside, and at the same time transforming the quality of their lives forever, by creating that unique place we call home.

Home

I've become disillusioned by the state of housing in Britain. Most house-builders are constructing the cheapest quality homes for maximum profit while we take on enormous mortgages to pay for them. The homes are not only built on the cheap, expensive to buy and environmentally unfriendly, they are also ugly, built in a mock-Georgian/Victorian/Tudor or neo-classical style that in no way reflects the way we live in the 21st century. They also look exactly the same as each other. You know the ones I mean – the tiny little Noddy boxes only inches apart from each other with tiny little gardens and tiny little cramped rooms inside. The sea of orangey-red roof tiles flooding our countryside breaks my heart. Ok, there is an enormous demand for new housing in Britain, I understand that, but why do we have to build such characterless, low-quality, ecologically damaging and badly designed homes that laden our lives with debt? I often look at these houses and think they look quite sad and depressed. For centuries we have built fantastic homes in this country; some could even be regarded as our national treasures. This book, *Build A New Life,* is all about restoring old buildings that are part of our history and heritage.

Your home is probably the most special place to you in the world; I know mine is for me. The French philosopher Gaston Bachelard wrote 'the house is one of the greatest powers of integration for the thought, memories and dreams of mankind'. I couldn't agree more. A

We have such a rich heritage of beautiful historic buildings just crying out for renovation.

home is far more than just bricks and mortar; it's a series of individual and personal spaces that contains so much about our everyday lives. It's where we wake up every day, where we eat, sleep, read, watch TV, drink, play, watch our kids grow up, where we laugh and cry. Often I think of my home as a personality, an extended member of the family, if you like, who provides shelter, warmth and protection for us from the world outside.

Our homes deserve to be buildings that are beautifully built, full of character and which reflect the individual lives of those who live within them. This is what *Build A New Life* is about — people creating wonderful, unique homes they have spent most of their lives dreaming of. This book will show you how to find, design and renovate your dream home on an affordable budget.

> # There's no place like home...
>
> Dorothy, *The Wizard of Oz*

People and place

For the past three years I've been lucky enough to follow over thirty families who've made the life-changing decision to leave their town or city behind and head for the country. They are people sick of the daily grind, of working every waking hour to pay the bills and finance the debt of their huge mortgages. They are exhausted by the hectic pace of city life, where work dominates their existence and family life suffers. After years of 'living' like this they hit a stage in their lives when enough was enough. Things *had* to change.

Most of us get no further than talking about such a move, but these people got on and did it, with incredible energy and focus. We're not just talking about people moving from one house to another. I see them as courageous British adventurers heading into the unknown. Just think about what most of these families are doing. They are selling their city or town houses, leaving their jobs, taking their kids out of school, often leaving behind family and friends to move to the countryside to find and renovate an old derelict property. Often they have no building experience whatsoever, but they get new jobs, put the kids into new schools, discover new friends and reduce their mortgage and living costs. This can happen in less than a year, which is unbelievable when you think about it. You could say that it's madness, but if you dream of being in a place where your quality of life

Feeling the lush green British countryside underfoot has to be better than city concrete.

This is your chance to create the type of home and lifestyle you really want, in a location you love.

will dramatically improve, then it's a risk you are willing to take. I can honestly say it's been a privilege to have followed so many wonderful life-changing stories, to have seen how good buildings in beautiful locations can make such a difference to the lives of those who build them. The contributors to the series have been an absolute inspiration to me and when I think about how much their lives have changed, it brings a smile to my face.

About this book

This book will show you how to manage the transition between city life and country life as successfully as possible, with tips to help you decide whether to live in the country, by the sea or in the British wilderness. It will also show you how to design the layout of your new home, manage the building process, make things run smoothly on site and hopefully enjoy the process at the same time.

My architectural practice has designed and built houses all over the world for our clients, but I wanted to include a chapter about a very small and simple home that I built for myself in the beautiful Dorset countryside (see Chapter 10). This was a very challenging project but illustrates what can be achieved with very little money, a lot of passion, hard work, determination, commitment and vision … oh and a dose of naivety!

If you dream of building a fantastic and unique home for your family in a stunning part of the British countryside then don't even think about it, just do it. It will be the adventure of a lifetime and I promise you will never regret it.

All adventurers need a good companion to guide them through uncharted waters. If you are brave enough to attempt to build a new life then I hope this book will help you to avoid the perils along the way and inspire you to maintain a steady course. Good luck!

WHY?
WHAT?
WHERE?
HOW?
WHO?
WHEN?

PLANNING A NEW LIFE

There are big decisions to make **when** you take the
plunge to Build a New Life. Have you truly examined
why you want to do this, **where** you want to be, and
what type of property would be your dream home?
In this section we'll look at what it really means to
live in the countryside, by the sea, or in remote and
splendid isolation.

Many of us dream of beginning a new life or transforming the way we live. We fantasise about a peaceful country existence when we're stuck in the city rush hour; we think about simpler ways of making money when we're chained to a high-pressured job; and we imagine the different lifestyle our family could lead in a quieter, more picturesque corner of Britain.

But few of us actually take the plunge. It's far easier to dream about that beautiful rural dwelling, drool over other people's renovation projects on television and read about how someone else created their dream home by the sea than it is to actually ditch our cramped city flat and jump in. We might crave a different quality of life, but we're too good at coming up with excuses as to why we shouldn't pursue the dream. I've heard so many people say that it's too expensive, impractical or just impossible to build a new life. Yet the reality, when you dig deeper, is that the majority of those people just don't know where to start. They're scared of taking risks and scared of the unknown, even if the familiar isn't making them happy. And they worry about what will happen if they put in all the graft and turn their lives upside down, only to discover that their new life isn't all they thought it would be. The biggest gamble of all is breaking their routine and giving up what they've got, even if they suspect that they could be getting much more out of life.

All of the brave British adventurers we've featured on *Build A New Life in the Country* have faced the same dilemmas. What often started as a daydream became an aspiration and finally an ambitious vision which they bought to life. But this, of course, didn't happen overnight. Most thought long and hard about how they really wanted their life to be – what their dream home would look like, how they wanted to live and how their life outside of work could be different.

In doing so they discovered that home became a central focus. They asked themselves what kind of location and landscape fulfilled their needs and what kind of property they really wanted to call home. And they considered the crucial questions of how they could achieve their goals, the most important of which was how they would fund their project. They had to consider which elements of their current lifestyle they wanted to lose and which they were desperate to hold on to. And then they had to be prepared for the challenges that such a radical change would inevitably bring.

With this in mind, this section of the book will help you to navigate your way around the big, fundamental questions behind the decision to leave an expensive and stressful city life for a simple, less demanding and often more family-orientated life in the country. It will get you thinking as to whether now is the right time for you to build a new life and, if so, where you should do it. Remember, too, that it's important to keep a focus on whose dream you're pursuing. Your decision needs to be right for everyone involved. If it's just your personal heaven, it could turn into your family's hell.

Chapter 1 will tell you what it's really like to live in a country town or village, Chapter 2 will focus on coastal living, and Chapter 3 will look at life out in the wilds. So that you can properly explore the options of each landscape, I'll spell out the pros and the cons to consider. And I'll illustrate all of this with case studies from the series so that you can see a selection of the kinds of properties, lifestyles and opportunities that country and seaside living can offer – the truly inspirational yet affordable homes and lifestyles that our families on *Build A New Life in the Country* carved out for themselves.

In short, this section of the book will help you to decide the 'why', 'what', 'where', how', 'who' and 'when' of building a new life.

CHAPTER ONE

Build a New Life in the Countryside

There is no doubt that the British countryside is a beautiful and desirable place to live today, but it hasn't always been that way. For centuries we considered our countryside to be 'bandit country' – wild, rugged terrain that was worked by the poor or inhabited by a wealthy elite – and the majority of us chose to live in the more 'civilised' towns and cities across the UK. Early writers such as Chaucer and Shakespeare described the worth of our landscape, but it wasn't until the romantic period began in the 18th century, inspired by the writings of Wordsworth and Byron, that we really began to see the natural beauty of our countryside rather than just revere it. Holiday-makers started to appreciate the wildlife, the benefits of fresh air and the varied and vast open terrain, seeing the country as an escape and a 'tonic' from their working lives, just as we do today. Literally millions of us flock to the Great Outdoors each weekend, only to return to our city lives on Sunday nights. So why not live permanently in the countryside? To decide that, you must consider carefully what are the benefits and pitfalls of living in the country today. This chapter will help you do that.

Many of us are rediscovering the benefits of having the Great British landscape on our doorstep, trading our built-up, urban views for open vistas and our proximity to shopping centres for a closeness to nature. Our countryside offers such a rich and varied landscape that we could choose between a sleepy village, lush green fields or a bustling market town in which to set up a new home. Then there are the areas of the country to consider, what type of property is commonly available there, and factors such as the climate, the cost of living, property prices, business

The British countryside has such a wonderful range of beautiful landscapes on offer.

prospects and facilities to take into account.

Across the series, our contributors chose a vast variety of destinations in which to build their new life. Matt and Emma Cupper chose the wilds of Lincolnshire, transforming a massive 18th-century granary with five acres of land into a home for themselves and their two young children, Cassie and Archie. Glyn and Jan Grayson decided to move to the heart of the Derbyshire countryside and renovated a beautiful old farmhouse just outside the village of Snelston. Meanwhile, David and Rebecca Palfrey ditched the Birmingham suburbs for a mortgage-free life in the heart of the Welsh countryside. The possibilities seem to be endless, so where do you start? The first step is to establish the kind of country living that you're after...

Country towns

Country towns are a good choice for those who want a quieter life without leaving behind all of the conveniences that city living offers, such as a good choice of schools, shops, pubs and restaurants, and perhaps a cinema or leisure centre too. You'll find most of these needs catered for in a country town, just on a smaller scale. You're likely to find that the local pub, shops and eateries are within walking or at least cycling distance. With lots going on, you'll be able to get involved in the community as well as keep yourself to yourself when you want to. Many towns offer good commuter links to neighbouring cities and a variety of opportunities for business, so you won't feel out of touch with the city life you've left behind. You can choose from historic towns, spa towns and market towns, according to what best suits you. But although you're more likely to have better access to the countryside than from the city, you might not necessarily feel more connected with nature if those wide, open spaces are still a good drive away.

A picturesque cottage is many people's idea of the perfect country village home.

Country villages

Villages offer a more intimate way of life than towns – everyone knows everyone, and their business too. Some people thrive on this; others find it stifling. Many of our villages are beautiful but, depending on your location, you might still find your immediate environment to be not so different from a town or city – you could still open your front door onto a busy road unless you're on the outskirts, have the luxury of land or a fantastic view. You can probably walk to the local shop, pub or post office but may find a car is vital to get to the open countryside or that amenities and transport links are limited.

Slightly off the beaten track

If you're craving a more rural way of life that's closer to nature than it is to neighbours, then living on the outskirts of a town or village might be for you. The advantages are a sense of real country living and a greater feeling of solitude, without being cut off. You'll just need to be ready to jump in the car whenever you need a pint of milk. If you want to be completely off the beaten track, turn to Chapter 3 where there is more about living in the wilds. In the meantime, here's how living in or just outside a village or country town could benefit you and your family.

Derby
Working Closer to Home

Many people dread their commute to work, but Glyn Grayson's daily journey was worse than most. He drove 250 miles to and from his demanding job as General Manager of a multi-million pound car window company in Bedford, and he'd been doing it for ten years. Jan, his wife, had given up running her own promotions business to be a wife and mother, but she felt Glyn had become a stranger in his own home, he spent so little time there. The couple finally decided they'd had enough of the long hours and the stress. They wanted a new life and a new home in an idyllic location, which they'd have more time to enjoy with their three-year-old daughter, Lydia.

Glyn and Jan found a huge, run-down farm in the heart of the Derbyshire countryside, complete with 12 acres, 7 outbuildings and a wrecked farmhouse. What a change! It couldn't have been more different from their home – a small, detached, developer-build property with a tiny garden on a banal housing estate.

In addition, their new dream property was only half an hour away from a new factory Glyn was opening, as well as being just half a mile from the picturesque village of Snelston. Glyn could see an end to his long commute and Jan was keen to exercise her passion for design in her new home. The couple planned to transform the outbuildings into holiday lets, to provide a second income.

It was a fantastic project – a perfect long-term plan for a stress-free life and the first home that Glyn and Jan would make together as a married couple.

When what turned out to be a very stressful project was finally complete, it looked stunning. After all they'd been

Their idyllic country home looked stunning and retained the historic details of the local architecture.

George, Jan and Glyn, midway through the project and still smiling...

through, Glyn decided to leave his job and call time on a ten-year relationship with the company he worked for, to work from home. The couple planned to turn another of their barns into a second holiday let to further increase their income. Finally, their life–work balance seemed right. The barn was not just the perfect home, but the key to their future together.

'I think we've realised a dream. It's 60 steps up the quality of life ladder,' said Jan.

The pros of country living

Improved quality of life, more quality time by yourself and with your family, a healthier, stress-free outdoor life among wildlife and nature, the chance to be part of a countryside community, not to mention more space for your money – there's no doubt there are plenty of reasons to leave city life behind.

Community life

Making the transition from being a city dweller to becoming part of a country community isn't always easy, but it can be very fulfilling – it just might not feel natural after years of urban living. You'll be used to anonymity, keeping yourself to yourself and not getting involved with other people's business. I've known people who've literally lived in the same city house for years and never known their neighbours.

I'm a city dweller. I always find people from my neighbourhood friendly, but also find that I rarely have the time to socialise with them or stop to chat on the street. City people who've moved to the country, however, find that they do have time to do these things. They feel part of what's going on in their immediate environment, sharing news, getting involved in local events and making new acquaintances.

If you choose to live in a close-knit community you'll find that the more effort you put into being part of country life, the more you will get out of it. Once you've settled in, it can be very rewarding to be in an environment where most people address you by your first name and know who you are. There's also a great tradition of people helping each other out, due to the lack of immediate amenities, which can prove to be invaluable both practically and in building relationships.

Some communities are more active than others, so whether you want a quiet life, or to be part of lots of local events, find out as much

as you can about the people and their social calendar via the Internet or by a visit to the local village or town hall before you decide on a particular town or village.

A stress-free life

For me, reducing stress is one of the most rewarding aspects of building a new life.

Many of the couples and families featured across the series felt that they had their life–work balance completely wrong when I first met them. Many had high-pressured jobs which had become detrimental to their health and family life. Others felt they had very little free time to themselves and most spent too much time feeling stressed.

Redressing the balance was often a catalyst for our contributors to make a life-changing move to discover a quieter, less work-orientated life. Many knew they had to change their priorities and put their health, home, leisure time and family before work, more of the time. Building a new life in the country allowed them to do just that: cutting their overheads enabled them to spend less time in the office or start a new, less frantic way of earning a living; reducing their bills and their cost of living by moving to the country gave them less of a financial burden; and spending more of their free time outdoors (rather than entertaining themselves in the city)

> ...the more effort you put into being part of country life, the more you will get out of it.

was not only better for their wallets, but also better for their health. I really did see a massive change in some of our contributors' lives by the time their project was complete.

A stress-free life in the country isn't a given, it's something to work towards. You will still need to fund your dream, however much you're downshifting. Are you happy to have less material wealth in return for a better quality of life? This is the time to ask yourself some serious questions about your career and what you consider to be a 'good standard of living' (see box below). Once you've decided *how* you're going to work, think about whether this will allow you to afford the kind of new life you're considering. How much money can you spend on mortgage repayments if you change your job or modify your career plans?

Wildlife, nature and animals

Part of building a new life is rethinking how you spend the majority of your free time. If you're passionate about nature, then country living could give you the opportunity to spend more time in the Great Outdoors and a slower pace of life to enjoy the change in seasons. Maybe, like Frank in Croatia (see page 67), you want to rekindle the passion you had for wildlife as a child. Or maybe you want to let your kids experience nature first hand rather than from a book or the TV. Before I built my Dorset house, the closest my kids got to wildlife in London were dirty foxes and pigeons. Now they can see fields of cows, spot rabbits in the garden and visit farms full of livestock nearby.

I hear so many parents say that living in the country has transformed what they do as a family. From walking nature trails to bird watching, or simply playing a game of rounders, country activities take the reliance away from the TV and video games. Many adults become inspired to get fit by the prospect of long country walks, or taking up a new sport. Others start a new hobby such as landscape painting, or get into cooking local, seasonal produce.

ASSESSING **LIFE–WORK BALANCE**

⌃ Would living in a less stressful environment allow you to feel calmer in your current job?

⌃ Should you consider taking a cut in salary to fund a quieter life with more free time and less of life's more costly luxuries?

⌃ Would working part-time cut your stress in half and enable you to pursue new opportunities in work and leisure?

⌃ Could you consider working from home or outside of a city office? How would that benefit you?

⌃ Do you crave a complete career change? Or could you use your skills in a different capacity, job or company that interests you?

Upwell, Cambridgeshire
Back to Nature

Tracy and Paul Fitzpatrick lived in a comfortable home in the suburbs of Herefordshire with their children. Tracy kept two horses and Paul worked in a shed at the bottom of their garden making luxury photo albums for sale in London boutiques, but their life was far from idyllic. To keep up their lifestyle, Tracy worked gruelling twelve-hour night shifts five days a week and seven- or eight-hour shifts every weekend. At the end of every shift, she'd drive for nearly an hour each way to go and feed her horses in a field that she rented. She'd been doing this for nine years.

Tracy was reaching burn out and dreamt of a different existence in the countryside. Paul longed to spend more quality time with his family, become part of a rural community and give his wife the life with nature she had always dreamed of. Eventually, he devised a plan to give Tracy, the family and the horses a healthier life. They would convert a disused apple store with 12 acres of land and stables for the horses in the Cambridgeshire Fens into their new home. I thought that the idea of transforming an agricultural apple store into a new home was brilliant.

The build didn't always run smoothly and Tracy had to continue working her shifts, but she came down to help Paul and stay in the caravan on site every weekend. She immediately felt the benefits of the countryside. 'This feels like home,' she said. 'Every Friday I think I'm going home, even though it's only a caravan, it's so relaxing once you get here … it's just like a permanent holiday.'

There were compromises to be made along the way to ensure the best for the horses – the stable block became an absolute priority of the build so the horses could have immediate shelter for the winter weather, and the 100-year-old orchard of 300 mature apple trees had to be cut down, as too many apples would have given the horses colic.

We all dream of the life we'd like to lead, but most of us don't dare do more than dream. Paul and Tracy took a big chance and went for it. As a result, they now have a wonderful home in the country.

Early on in the project – building site with obligatory caravan as temporary home.

After much hard work and stress, Paul and Tracy had an imposing and bright home to feel proud of.

If you're lucky, your new home might come with a sizeable plot of land.

Family life

Many of our contributors felt that city living came at the expense of family life. Tracy Fitzpatrick in Cambridge had missed her three daughters' first teeth and seeing them walk for the first time because she'd had to spend so much time at work. Many parents across the series felt the same, as did couples who rarely saw each other due to their busy lives. They decided to swap spending such limited time together, when they were stressed and tired, for more quality time as a family. They wanted to be there to pick up the children from school before organising a big family meal where everyone could chat about their day. In short, to generally do more together as a unit and enjoy each other's company.

An affordable life

Buying a bigger house doesn't always mean increasing your mortgage and therefore your debt. It's still possible to find pockets of beautiful British countryside where property prices are an absolute steal compared to those in commuter towns and city locations in high demand. To get a family-sized home for a really good price you'll probably need to take on a renovation project to make the property work for you, but despite the spend, you could still be quids in if you're both clever and careful (see page 117 on how to budget for your build).

And it's all worth it. Cutting your debt and the size of your mortgage is a big stress-buster. It can allow you to finally live within your means rather than feel that you're forever chasing the next cheque to pay off another chunk of debt. You can re-think your life–work balance – maybe one person in a couple can give up work, maybe both can work part-time or, with a little cash in your pocket from the sale of a city home, perhaps you can start a new business to fund your new life. My advice is to always do your sums properly. Carefully calculate what you might make from the sale of your current property and how much you'd need to spend moving to the country without stretching yourself on the property ladder. Get quotes from estate agents on the value of your current home and start looking at property papers to see what you can comfortably afford.

Building a new life isn't about taking on bigger debts, it's about creating an affordable life. Depending on how you restructure your working life, you'll probably find you can spend less on business lunches, business suits and taxis, for example. Shopping locally could provide you with cheaper, fresher and often better-quality local produce than you'd find at supermarkets. You can cut out those takeaways you relied on when you were too tired from work to cook, those expensive beers in city bars and high-priced cinema tickets. But be realistic about how much extra you might need to spend on petrol and car maintenance, your potential cut in earnings or the costs of running and setting up your own business. It's worth making an exhaustive list of your potential outgoings and savings and compare them to your current expenditure. You might find your dream is more attainable than you thought.

Lincolnshire
Focus on the Family

When people leave their old life behind to start afresh, they're usually looking for something better, but Matt and Emma Cupper seemed, on the surface, to have everything most people aspire to – a lovely house in a pretty village surrounded by friends and family. So why did they want to build a new life in the country?

The Cuppers' plan was to sell their small two-bed bungalow in Surrey for a bigger house and a simpler, more family-orientated life. They wanted some land and to have more children and a bigger property, but knew that doing that in Surrey, where house prices were escalating, would be impossible.

For the price of a bungalow in Surrey, they were able to buy a massive 18th-century granary in the Lincolnshire countryside with five acres of land to transform into their dream home. And they could afford all of it on Matt's income, allowing Emma to give up work at a local café in order to become a full-time mum to their two children.

The build wasn't easy – Emma confessed she had 'never imagined it would be so tough' – and Matt felt the pressure of the schedule, the dwindling budget and doing most of the work himself. But the kids were instantly happy at their new nursery on a working farm and before the project was even complete Emma had some fantastic news – she discovered that she was pregnant again.

Once their new home was finished, Emma decided to create a bit of 'the good life' and get a vegetable patch growing and some chickens, while she looked after the children and Matt returned to work. Matt and Emma managed to fulfil their dreams of a new, simpler life focused around their family. Their new home and lifestyle was everything they'd hoped for.

'[The house] is part of my heart, my soul really,' says Matt. 'At the end of the day I've given a lot of energy to this place for Emma, the children and myself, as a family. We want to live in it, enjoy it, spend time in it together, appreciate it and grow into it.'

George with Matt and Emma, taking a break from the pressures of the build.

The restored granary was imposing, and full of space and light.

Wales
The Dream of Mortgage-free Living

David and Rebecca were fed up with their lives being ruled by paying the mortgage. They left their teaching jobs, sold their suburban home near Birmingham and moved to a remote corner of Wales with their two young children. They were willing to gamble everything they had to live their rustic dream in the heart of the country and enjoy a debt-free life.

The couple had shared the dream of living in Wales for ten years, and had just found the perfect property when I met them – a beautiful, but derelict, barn that had at one time been used as a village hall. It had stunning views and an acre of land set in its own wooded glade.

David and Rebecca envisaged transforming the property into a rustic family home but without a huge mortgage, so they could afford a quieter life. They borrowed £100,000 with which to buy the property and wanted to spend as little as possible on the renovation. I thought this sounded like a great idea until I realised that they only had access to an incredibly small budget of just £12,000 for their ambitious project. With doors and windows to fit, electrics and plumbing to install, a leaky roof to patch and floorboards to lay, their budget was minimal to say the least. Yet David and Rebecca were determined to build their new home and a new life for their family.

David gave up work for a year to focus on the build and look after their kids Ellie and Tom, while Rebecca supported the family with her part-time job as a speech therapist. More time with the kids was all part of the dream, but David found that juggling the project with childcare slowed up progress as he attempted to do most of the work himself.

The budget for the build soon dwindled. But just as the entire project looked like it might be in financial jeopardy, David and Rebecca discovered that they could be sitting on the answer to their prayers. If they managed to get planning permission for someone to build on it, they could sell the piece of land beside their barn for approximately £50,000 – more than enough to cover their current costs and complete

Midway through the build, the Palfreys realised they would need more room for their growing brood.

The barn may have been derelict but it clearly had potential to be a great space.

The restoration brought out all the best features of the original building, such as the lovely exposed beams.

The Palfrey's use of natural materials throughout was perfect for the house.

their project. Planning permission is never granted overnight, so as a buffer they applied for a £20,000 loan so work could continue on the barn. They had to work longer hours to pay it off, but they tried to get the balance right between working to meet the deadlines for repayments and pushing the project forward. David ploughed ahead with the barn conversion.

Finally the couple received planning permission and an estate agent's valuation of up to £110,000 for the land. If they sold the plot for this amount, they could pay off their mortgage completely. Great news, but with no buyer, they decided to call in the professionals to fit windows and try to make the barn watertight as the winter weather took its toll on site. Meanwhile, the family received wonderful news – Rebecca was pregnant with their third child.

David and Rebecca finally completed the barn for £65,000 – way over their original budget. But luckily, they were also offered £75,000 for the plot of land, which would clear their debt and put them in a position to afford their new mortgage. Despite running out of money during the project, they ended up with a unique and charming home with tons of character, and they could look forward to an affordable life with more time for their family. They finally managed to set themselves up with the lifestyle they'd always dreamed of and could comfortably sustain.

Even on the smallest budget, the Palfreys still managed to create a unique and charming home.

THE **PROS OF** COUNTRY LIVING

- ⋏ Community life
- ⋏ Stress-free living
- ⋏ At one with nature
- ⋏ Improved family life
- ⋏ An affordable life
- ⋏ Improved quality of life
- ⋏ More time

Quality of life

If you feel as though you're missing out on the important and enjoyable things that life has to offer because you're always working to pay the bills and fund a life in the city, then you have a lot in common with many of the contributors featured across the series. But what do you consider 'quality of life' to be? If you crave more space than is currently offered by your built-up environment, more time to do the hobbies and activities you enjoy, a more relaxed pace and a greater focus on the family, then a new life in the country could be just what you need.

Time

Almost everyone who was filmed for the series said that they were so glad that they didn't wait any longer to build a new life. In fact, most said, 'I wish I'd done this years ago.' Their universal cry was, 'you only live once, don't wait, do it now!'

Time is so precious, it's too easy to let years go by while you're immersed in a hectic job, only taking a break for a holiday twice a year. What a waste! You might miss your kids growing up, like Tracy and Paul in Upwell did, or miss out on the chance to pursue the affordable way of life you've always dreamt of, which was what David and Rebecca in Wales

feared would happen to them. At the very least you owe it to yourself to put a two-, five- or ten-year plan into place, which you can revisit again in a year or two's time and see what might be possible, whatever your personal situation.

Of course, not all of your worries will melt away when you move to the countryside and you shouldn't think that building a new life in the country will solve all of the problems you currently experience in the city. The initial move can be very highly stressful and any subsequent building project can test the character and strength of your marriage and family life. It's important, therefore, to see the big picture and that means looking at the obstacles, down sides and harsh realities of living in the country.

Your quality of life is so much to do with the nature of your immediate environment.

The cons of country living

You've found the beautiful house, in the dream location. You're incredibly excited and can't wait to move in and decorate. Then you find you don't know a soul and not all the locals seem too keen to make friends. What's more, you can't do anything without the car and in winter all the roads are blocked by snow.

Let's take a realistic look at some of the difficulties you might experience when you start to build a new life in the country.

A shock to the system

Living a rural life can be a shock if you've spent many years in the city. At first you might feel that there's not much happening in your immediate location, but you need to give yourself time to get used to doing different things and to adjust to a slower pace of life. Is it really worth getting frustrated if you're stuck behind a tractor when you don't have a business meeting to get to in ten minutes' time? Does it matter if you can't get the latest blockbuster at the nearest cinema when you've got an amazing view and the summer months to enjoy some outdoor living? It's all about leaving the city behind. Literally. Some contributors told me that for weeks after moving to their new home they could still hear the buzz of the city beyond their actually silent front door, as if the endless hum of the city had followed them. Others found the quiet unnerving. These things are just all part of the readjustment – it's important to embrace what's different about your new location and enjoy it, rather than focus on what you could be doing elsewhere.

The British countryside is beautiful but the isolation may take some getting used to.

To do this, you really have to make a concerted effort to adjust your mindset and consciously make a decision not to get worked up about things. If you manage it, you'll feel as though you've left a huge amount of stress behind you.

Tight-knit communities

A common complaint I heard when filming the series was that some contributors felt that they'd never fit into their new community. Some small towns and villages are very close knit and include inhabitants who've lived there for generations. A small place, where everyone knows everyone else, can seem impenetrable at first, but the key is to really make an effort. You need to be visible in your new community and that means getting involved in village events such as fetes, shopping locally, drinking in the pub and meeting your immediate neighbours. You'll naturally meet people when you take the kids to school, if you join a local club or take a local job. But if these aren't options for you then at the very least knock on your neighbour's door to introduce yourself. They'll be naturally curious about you and interested to meet you. You'll be living relatively close to just a few people, so life will be made easier if you make the effort to get along. Neighbours in the country can be as

Are you ready to swap the busy sounds of city life for the peace and tranquillity of the country?

fantastic or as undesirable as those in the city, but in a small community a fall-out can have a greater impact.

Some local communities can be very old-fashioned or have their own ways of doing things, which, as a newcomer, you'll need to respect. Don't confuse trying to fit in with taking over existing systems – this could make you enemies. You're the newcomer and it's for you to fit in with how things are done, even if you don't agree with everything.

Until you make a new set of friends and feel at home with your neighbours, it's common to miss friends and family from your old life. I found that the contributors who travelled back to their old home town or to stay with family regularly found it took much longer to fit into their new community in the long run. Just get on with it!

You'll know it when you've become part of the local community and there will still be things you won't have quite got your head around. I've heard several of the contributors say they'd always dreamt of living with the back door open, so that neighbours could wander in and out freely, like in the 1950s and '60s. But when they ended up making 15, sometimes

THE CONS

- A shock to the system
- Tight-knit communities
- The Great British weather
- The myth of more time

20 cups of tea a day for people dropping by and couldn't get a thing done, it drove them around the bend.

The Great British weather

Yes, we are a nation obsessed with the weather. Let's face it, we can't stop talking about it. But when you're living in the country, there's good reason to. You probably don't need me to tell you that you'll be more exposed to the elements when you live in the country, but you might be shocked to find out how much the weather can dominate and dictate what you can get up to. The wind, rain, snow and cold have a greater impact on your lifestyle, and the winter months are the longest in the British calendar year. You need to learn to be hardy. If you want to keep pigs you need to be prepared to round them up when they escape on yet another cold, dark,

rainy evening. If you dream of romantic open fires, are you happy to chop logs throughout the winter in all conditions, so that you can keep everyone warm? Will it be a disaster for your business if you're snowed in? Of course spring, summer and autumn can be wonderful in the country and you can literally wake up and watch as the seasons change, which is amazing in itself, but remember how much of the year is warm and sunny, and think about how the remaining months will make you feel.

One lady we featured on the series told me that she felt as though she'd been 'conned' by the Scottish weather. Every time she went up to the Highlands to look at properties for sale in the area the weather was so bright and sunny, she said it duped her into buying. She visited a wreck on a glorious day and thought it would be fine living in a caravan on a pretty, sunny site.

Remember what the winter months can bring. Can you cope with your new life all year round?

But from the day she made the move up to Scotland the weather was terrible and made her feel miserable.

The myth of more time

Unless you've given up work or are very organised, you won't automatically have more time in the country just because you've moved there. You'll still be picking up the kids, doing the housework, the shopping and the chores. If you buy a larger house, it will require more maintenance and cleaning time and a garden will keep you busy. In addition, if you're working in a neighbouring town or city, you might spend more time than you had previously travelling to and from work or to amenities. While you might find all of these things more pleasurable in a country setting, it's important to be realistic about the amount of free time you will have and to be relaxed when some things in the country take longer to get done.

The aim is to allow yourself a life where you can make more free time for the things you love – and for the people you want to spend it with. In the meantime, enjoy taking more time to do the basic things in life – like shopping for fresh, seasonal produce locally, at a country pace.

The view from your window will be a million miles from your old city outlook.

Just think how much better this feels than your old dash round the supermarket and how much more beneficial your new shopping regime is for local trade, the farmers and the environment.

Starting to build a new life

Once you've decided that you want to live in or on the outskirts of a country town or village, go there and explore it thoroughly. This is how I found my own home in the countryside. I spent

TOP RESEARCH TIPS

- ⌃ Consult property papers and local newspapers.
- ⌃ Look at community noticeboards.
- ⌃ Ring on someone's bell – the direct approach!
- ⌃ Exploit the potential of the Internet.
- ⌃ Find out about local schools and facilities.
- ⌃ Talk to the Council Planning Department.

hours and hours driving around an area that I'd fallen in love with.

The only way to find out which part of the country you want to live in is to get a real feel for a variety of places you're drawn to. This may be because you've visited a certain part of the country before and loved it, because you have a connection there, have read about a place or have had it recommended to you. While you're there you can explore the whole area – not just the trendy, popular and therefore expensive parts. Look at the quirkier, sleepier villages or up-and-coming and hidden towns on the outskirts where you might find a bargain.

Pick up the property papers, the local newspaper, and get a sense of the community and how quiet or busy it seems. I'd suggest that if you decide it might be the place for you, keep your eyes open not only for 'For Sale' signs, but also pluck up the courage to walk up and knock on the door of your dream property. This really is one of my biggest tips – be bold, ring the bell, apologise for the intrusion, tell them what you're up to and flatter the homeowner by asking them to get in touch with you should they ever want to sell. I know it seems odd, but at the very least it's a good way of meeting someone who might become your neighbour. I found the property we turned into our home in Dorset this way and we got a better deal direct than going through estate agents (see page 160 for the complete story). It works!

When you're back home you can reflect on how the area you visited made you feel and consider what it might be like living there. Do some more research into its history, its social calendar and schools and amenities on the Internet, and contact the local planning department for a list of run-down or condemned buildings that might be ideal for renovation.

Once you've set your heart on a specific place, start thinking about how to square the

> # Contact the local planning department for a list of run-down buildings.

dream of the area you've fallen for with the reality of what you can afford. You might find you need to make some compromises. Say, for example, that you love fishing. You long to live on the edge of a lake in a beautiful part of the countryside, but you can't afford the reality of *all* of these elements. An hour's drive to the lake, through stunning scenery, may be the compromise you need to make in order to be able to tick the other boxes.

The one resource that will help you reach these kinds of decisions – by showing you exactly what's on offer, for how much and where – is the Internet. It has radically transformed house-buying today. You can tap in the name or postcode of an area of the country in which you want to search and all of a sudden you've got a list of estate agents operating in the immediate surroundings.

This may all sound obvious, but you must exhaust the possibilities, weigh up different areas of the country by physically visiting them and by using the technology now available to search in one part of the country while you're living in another. Buying property is one of the single biggest investments we ever make and our home is vital to the way we choose to live. If the process of finding where to move next takes some time, so be it, at least you'll be happy with your final decision.

CHAPTER TWO

Build a New Life by the Sea

The British coastline is one of our most treasured, national assets. But it wasn't until the 18th century that the seaside resort was invented. With the advent of the industrial revolution, the wealthy were able to take respite from the cities and went in search of the health benefits of the sea air. The seaside became a popular place to go on holiday and by the end of the century the development of the railways, marketing campaigns and the advent of facilities available in London, accelerated a boom in the popularity of resorts such as Brighton and St Ives. Sunbathing, sport, fresh air and sea views became as popular as they remain today.

The dream of living by the sea is one that most of us can understand. Wouldn't it be wonderful if the sea was the first thing you opened your eyes to every morning? Wouldn't you love to hear the sound of the waves rolling onto the beach and seagulls soaring overhead as you relaxed in your living room? And when you went to buy your daily paper, see the fishing boats heading back to the port with a catch in their nets? You could keep a little boat yourself, moored within walking distance, to tinker about on. You could spend evenings dining shore-side, enjoying the view and a cold glass of wine with friends. You could walk barefoot across golden sandy beaches with your partner and build sandcastles with your kids. But how close is the romanticised dream of coastal living to the reality of daily life by the sea? And how do you know what kind of seaside living is out there or might be right for you?

Britain has some wonderfully dramatic coastline, where waves crash against rocky cliffs.

THE SEASCAPES

- Rocky, rugged coastlines
- Elegant cliffs and bays with flat sandy beaches for the kids to play on
- Small fishing villages
- Bustling coastal towns
- Traditional English seaside resorts
- Wild and remote coastal outposts

A wide expanse of beach with gentle waves is perfect for strolling and relaxation.

There are so many beautiful and inspiring places along our coastline that it can be difficult to know where to start. My advice is to begin by concentrating on two main factors in tandem: a) what you want out of your location in terms of lifestyle and b) what you need from your location to make your dream work financially.

But first there's a very simple question to answer – what kind of coastal living are you craving? Think about the huge variety of coastal landscapes on offer and carefully consider which will suit you best (see box opposite).

Where to start your search will also depend on your particular financial situation. If the boom of more popular resorts means that prices have been pushed out of your reach, or if your business will be dependent on water sports, boats, tourists or other elements, you need to ensure these things are in plentiful supply at your chosen destination. Whatever your situation or the compromises you might need to consider, building a new life by the sea can give you an incredible outdoor lifestyle which can really give a boost to your quality of life. If it's peace and tranquillity that you're after, remote coastal living might be for you (see Case Study page 34).

The pros of living by the sea

You may be dreaming of watching your kids comb the sands for crabs and shells, or setting up the perfect B&B. Or you might yearn for an isolated life on a bleak and windswept cliff, or even restoring your own barge and transforming it into a home afloat. Seaside living offers many exciting opportunities, as you'll see from the experiences of our contributors.

The Isle of Seil
Renovating an Unusual Building

When I first met Paul and Margaret Drew, who were planning to set up a coastal B&B, I wondered why they weren't considering popular coastal resorts in Devon, Cornwall or somewhere warm on the south coast. They were quick to respond: 'There are people there! Lots of them!' Seeking solitude was a vital part of their dream. 'We like being on our own,' said Margaret, 'not in a crowd. Somewhere where you just sit there and hear nothing.'

Paul and Margaret yearned for a slower, more old-fashioned way of life. So with a 'now or never' attitude, they upped sticks and moved over 400 miles from their home in Sheffield to live a relaxed, solitary life on a spectacular island just off the west coast of Scotland. The sleepy Isle of Seil offered all they were craving – a stunning landscape, just 500 inhabitants and access to the mainland via a beautiful 18th-century stone bridge.

The Drews faced a compromise – the only way they could afford their dream on the island was to renovate a dilapidated property and use part of it as a business. They bought a 100-year-old corrugated iron church to transform into their home and a small B&B business, allowing them both to retire from full-time work as GP's receptionist and electrician.

The building is a very rare and unique part of our industrial heritage – one of the earliest examples of pre-fabricated architecture and a revolutionary building for a church. Churches traditionally took years to build and were crafted from stone and brick in a very decorative and ornate fashion. But this was the first truly industrial church.

When the church was built in 1911, for a mere £100, it was designed to serve as a temporary structure until more church funds were found, and was delivered as a self-assembly kit ready to be erected by the parishioners. But the building was never replaced and has stood for nearly 100 years. It was way ahead of its time and beyond anything even Ikea have come up with!

The church cost Paul and Margaret £80,000, leaving them just £70,000 to live off and to fund their renovation.

I'll never forget looking at the building from the outside the first time I visited the couple and wondering why they didn't just knock the property down and start again. But Paul would joke, 'basically I'm a

The unique pre-fabricated 'tin church'.

Yorkshireman and I like to recycle anything I can – I'm really mean!' But when I went inside, it all made sense – the space was fantastic. It did need a lot of work, however: a new corrugated shell and wooden structure for the whole building, a new first floor and the construction of a complete working house.

This was a self-build project, which Paul and Margaret aimed to complete in just eight months – by July, so that they could cash in on the short holiday season for their let. They planned to do all the work themselves, but soon realised that this would be beyond them, especially the heavy work, which Margaret wouldn't be able to manage. So they enlisted the help of another Englishman living on the island, Tony. 'If you knew all of the problems beforehand, you probably wouldn't take it on,' Paul confessed.

At first Margaret enjoyed some well-deserved leisure time while the men got on with most of the heavy work on the build. She ordered materials and looked after the accounts, but she also had time to appreciate her new lifestyle. She started to keep chickens and bake her own bread. In the evenings the couple were happy to cosy-up in their caravan with music, the local paper and a 'wee dram', as Margaret described it. It was all part of their slower pace of life.

Then bad weather, short winter days and dwindling finances put pressure on the build. Determined not to take on a mortgage or a loan, Margaret took on a job at the local launderette to keep the pennies rolling in and insulated the whole house with the help of her daughter, Sally.

For more on Paul and Margaret's project see pages 91, 122–3.

The building needed an entire new wooden structure, new corrugated shell and new first floor.

In its remote island setting, Paul and Margaret's dream home was not easily missed.

Paul and Margaret dreamed of a life of complete isolation – and that's exactly what they got!

Beach huts are a familiar sight on our seafronts. Run-down ones can still be picked up for very little.

Remote coastal living

If you like the idea of spending hours fishing, pottering on boats and going on scenic coastal walks without being able to spot a tourist for miles, you'll be the kind of person who wants to enjoy an unspoilt setting, away from the hubbub of built-up areas. You'll either be thinking of running a business from home or not working at all, and you'll be prioritising spending time with the family or your partner. For more benefits – as well as some downsides – of living a remote life, turn to Chapter 3.

Beach life

A life on the British coast is no longer just for those seeking retirement. In recent years, more and more young professionals, families and couples have fled the cities for the coast, to pursue a more outdoor-based life, enjoy the beach, sport and the benefits of the sea air. It's no coincidence that, in addition, many of our bustling seaside towns and villages now also offer some of the very best attractions that we tend to associate with our major cities.

For arts there's the Baltic Gallery in Newcastle, The De La Warr Pavilion in Bexhill-on-Sea, the Tate gallery in St Ives and the regeneration of the arts in Margate. For food, the standards often found in the very best city restaurants can now be found on the coast, where 'just-caught' fish and the freshest local produce are served, What's more, a host of celebrity chefs have set up flagship restaurants by the sea, including John Burton-Race's Carved Angel in Dartmouth and Jamie Oliver's Fifteen Cornwall in Watergate Bay. Some of our coastal towns, such as Leith in Edinburgh, have enjoyed incredible regeneration programmes. And the surf culture of Newquay has attracted thousands of young people who practise the sport they love by day and party by night.

Beach life is great for families. Kids love paddling, swimming and playing in the sand and searching for crabs, shells and fish. And the more time they spend doing this, rather than sat in front of the TV, the better in my book. The beach also gives families the opportunity to spend time together having fun,

Worthing
On the Waterfront

Web designer Gez Glover and barrister Laura Turner spent their twenties working hard in London, but city living took its toll and the capital soon lost its appeal. They eventually decided to sell their tower-block flat and move to the south coast in search of a beach lifestyle.

The sleepy seaside town of Worthing wouldn't have been the first choice for Gez and Laura to build their new life, but the couple managed to find a plot for sale right on the beach – a rare opportunity in the UK. They realised that if they grabbed the land, they could build themselves a great new home with uninterrupted views of the sea. The plot, however, didn't come cheap.

They bought the land for £300,000 – a lot more than they could afford – but immediately sold off half the plot to someone who would build their own home alongside theirs. As a result, they got a fantastic deal on their plot and with the £175,000 from the other plot they were able to file a planning application for the construction of their new seaside house.

The planning process, on such an exposed and sensitive site, was slow and difficult.

The couple waited three years for planning permission to be granted and when it came, strict, conditional rules meant that both builds had to happen simultaneously and would need to use the same materials. Undeterred, Gez and Laura embarked on an ambitious and impressive design, which stretched their budget to the limit, but which would result in a fantastic modern, glass-fronted beach house when complete.

Gez and Laura still wanted to pursue their careers, but what they were able to do with their free time radically changed as a result of their move. They cycled their bikes on the downs, Gez took up kite surfing and Laura started horse-riding lessons. 'We work hard and it's nice to have something to escape to,' said Laura the day I met her after riding. 'This is one of the things that I said I'd like to be able to do and I'm starting to do it. I'd never ever have been able to do this in London.'

Their dream of living on the beach did have a compromise attached. On the beach side of the house they have the most fantastic sea view, but on the other, they're on the busy Old Brighton Road. Yet for them it wasn't an issue.

George with Gez and Laura. Their new home could not have been closer to the sea.

The house backed onto a busy road, but the couple felt the proximity to the sea more than compensated.

'It's a small price to pay for the ability to be able to open the front doors and be straight onto the beach – kite surfing, canoeing, anything we want to do. That's what it was all about, changing from our city life to the coast. We don't see it as a problem, because you open the doors and there's your playground,' said Gez. The couple also spent money making sure that the back end of the house and the windows were highly insulated against the noise of the traffic.

Gez and Laura loved the outdoor life they moved to the coast for, but when the build got tough Gez found that working on his web design business full time as well as the build left him exhausted, and Laura ended up working flat out at her job as a barrister to bring in more money in order to fund the project. Suddenly, they found that they couldn't enjoy the very activities they'd made the move for. 'We haven't spent the weekends going over the downs and doing the normal things you want to do on a sunny day … we're working, and when we're not working we're doing something on the house and there is always something to do,' said Laura. 'In a sense we've lost some of

Gez and Laura's contemporary home stood out as an architectural statement on the seafront.

our normal life together. But it's temporary. Once we're in that house it won't matter in the slightest. The day we move in and I sit there on our balcony and have a drink, looking out over the sea, knowing I don't have to leave that building again, our whole lives will change immediately, and I think we'll forget everything that went before it. It's got to be worth it.'

Building your own home can be tiring, emotional and stressful, but in the end your sense of achievement is incredible.

For more on Gez and Laura's project see page 144.

The dramatic three-storey space, awaiting the delivery of the new staircase.

British beaches are currently cleaner than they've been for many years.

whether it's taking up a sport as a family, such as canoeing, or simply heading for the beach to make sandcastles or buy ice creams.

Now is a great time to build a new life by the sea. This is because British beaches are currently cleaner than they've been for many years. There was a period in the late 1970s and '80s when we were guilty of neglecting our coastlines, but happily, today's standards are high and we've cleaned up our act considerably. I'm always proud to see that the majority of people who visit our coastline are careful to pick up their litter and mindful of coastal paths.

Your own home afloat

Barge living is a Great British eccentricity and a wonderful way to relax and watch the world go by from the comfort of your own home. In the summer you can see beautifully painted barges trug up locks and canals at a snail's pace, while their owners lie back on deck and take in the scenery from their homes on the water. By wintertime, the barges' cosy interiors offer an escape from the winter weather on the sea. Traditionally in this country barges have been

Another type of coastal living – a typical Cornish high street with its bustling tourist shops.

mostly the preserve of holidaymakers, especially on areas such as the Norfolk Broads. Today, however, more and more people are opting to make their floating home their main residence and enjoy the real change of lifestyle that barge living can offer.

THE **PROS OF** LIFE BY THE SEA

- ⌃ The variety of lifestyles on offer – remote coast, family beach resorts, barge living
- ⌃ Ideal for watersports enthusiasts
- ⌃ Great potential for setting up your own B&B
- ⌃ Opportunity to take advantage of the considerable numbers of seasonal visitors
- ⌃ Perfect de-stressing environment

Gweek
Barge Living

Simon and Carol Morley left their comfortable family home in Cambridge and moved 400 miles to the Cornish coast. They wanted to start a new dive charter business from scratch and create a family home from an 80-ft barge moored in the sleepy Cornish village of Gweek. They both took redundancy from their stressful jobs in IT and used part of the cash to buy their barge for £90,000.

When they first bought it, the barge was, in Simon's words, like 'a country pub done bad'. I'd certainly never seen so much timber effect! It had been converted into basic accommodation by its previous owner, but to turn it into a comfortable family home required a complete overhaul. The two bedrooms were barely habitable.

The former workshop at the front of the barge had to be transformed into an open-plan living room and kitchen. To achieve their dream of space and light, Carol and Simon needed to rip out everything from their floating rust bucket and start again.

The wheelhouse would become an office with 360-degree views of the deck. Down below in the rear of the barge there would be a utility room, family bathroom and master bedroom. The kids' bedrooms would be totally transformed. But it was in the open-plan living space that they would blow most of their budget and create the centrepiece – a handmade, curved oak kitchen.

It was an ambitious plan, especially on their budget. After buying the barge the couple were left with £70,000. They earmarked £40,000 to set up their business, leaving just £30,000 to convert the barge and to live on until money from the business started to roll in. They gave themselves four months to get the barge totally restored with just £15,000 (and using the other £15,000 to live on while the work was being done).

With three kids, a dog and two cats it was absolute chaos for the family on their floating building site. And Simon found that

Carol and Simon's pride and joy: the 'Classic Lass' moored in its tranquil harbour setting.

George with Carol, Simon and the kids. A world away from their old high-pressure IT jobs.

DIY on a boat takes much longer than DIY on dry land. 'This is a real old boat and the whole thing is slightly bent anyway, that was the design of them. You don't get any straight edges, you certainly don't get any right angles. What it means is that you can measure one side and cut it to length and it's never straight, it's a real pain,' he told me. They also spent £600 of their budget on an industrial machine to remove the rust on the inside of the hull, something they didn't anticipate having to do. What's more, the couple had a setback when the boat sprang a leak, and a hold-up on the start of work on their hand-made kitchen meant they had to cancel their order for their dream, bespoke, curved units. They simply didn't have the time to wait for them to be made. They needed to start earning an income. Work stopped on the barge while they shifted their focus.

Simon set to work with business partner and best friend Spike Abrahams. They invested in a boat and plotted the wrecks and ruins they would take divers to. Then, they tried desperately to attract customers. Simon loved his new job. 'It's a 14-hour working day, but for a lot of it, you're playing about, you're on a boat, or you're diving. People pay money to go and do that,' he said. But with the season almost over, and without any marketing, the customers just didn't come. Eventually Simon and Spike took the dive boat out of the water, while Carol took a job selling door to door to literally keep them afloat.

Meanwhile, the kids were loving their new life. Josh, 10, and Georgia, 6, loved the local village school. Josh's school had just 30 pupils. He knew the names of everyone there and quickly made close

What a mess! This is what life was like for the Morleys when they first moved into their barge.

Money ran out for the hand-made kitchen so the family settled for standard, inexpensive units.

friendships. In particular he loved the after-school sailing classes. It was a world away from the life they'd left behind. 'If we were back in Cambridge now, Josh would probably be playing a games console or watching TV, possibly playing at a friends' house, but nothing like this. We're so pleased that this is part of his life now and he looks forward to this every week. How often do you see a head teacher up to their knees in water?!' said Carol. 'I think Josh's new school will transform his childhood.'

In the run-up to Christmas, however, the pressure of this project got too much and the couple unfortunately made the decision to split up. Undeterred, Carol bravely decided to push on alone, with the help of builders. She was absolutely focused and determined to pursue her dream of finishing the barge and creating a wonderful home on water for herself and her kids – and that's what she did. I really admired her determination, drive and all that she went through to pursue her dream.

'The smell of the seaside, the water is so clean and so clear, the beaches are clean, it just doesn't get better than this. Worries? What worries? This is just all worth it', said Carol of her new life on the sea.

Carol's story is also a reminder that if you're building a new life with a partner, your relationship has to be strong to survive the pressure. It's an amazing thing to do to improve your quality of life together, but if your relationship is under pressure already, the chances are that building a new life will make things worse and not better. See Chapter 9 for help on managing personal relationships under the pressure of the build.

When it all got too much, at least the Morleys could step outside and unwind on deck.

The hull was transformed from a 'country pub gone bad', as Simon put it, to a modern, light-filled space.

Carol's Aga – proof that you can enjoy traditional home comforts even on a barge.

B&B Britain

It's a Great British dream, running a Bed & Breakfast by the sea. This type of coastal living can be a wonderful way to get your hands on a larger property than you could ordinarily afford, have your paying guests help you meet the mortgage repayments and fund a seaside lifestyle. It can also be a way to work fewer hours (in a trade-off for being on call all of the time) and to have a stream of people bring your home to life. You can run a very profitable little business by the sea if you get it right, but you should know what's involved, how to put your dream into action, the tips and pitfalls before you think about drawing up that business plan. You need to think carefully about whether you are the type of person who can adopt a 'nothing's a problem' attitude all of the time, and you need to have researched your area carefully. If you're relocating to a popular tourist destination do you have a plan that will make your place really stand out from the large number of B&Bs already established there? (See what Peter and Andrea did with their St Ives B&B on page 46).

The questions below should get you thinking about all that's involved in running a B&B and enable you to decide whether this type of coastal living will work for you.

The ultimate relaxation

Spending time by the sea is a wonderful way to de-stress. It doesn't get much better than a stroll along the beach to wind down at the end of the day, or sitting and looking out to sea to clear your head and take respite from city life. It's almost impossible not to experience a sense of escapism, freedom and tranquillity – it must be something to do with that huge expanse of sky, the seemingly endless horizon and the mesmerising rhythm of the waves on the shore. It's uplifting, calming and good for our health.

IS B&B LIVING **FOR YOU?**

- Can you fund the purchase of a commercial property?
- Are you happy to be on call 24 hours a day?
- Will you enjoy opening your doors to a variety of different people and put on a welcoming smile all of the time?
- Are you prepared for your B&B to turn into a full-time job where you spend all day cleaning bedrooms and bathrooms?
- Do your family commitments fit in with this kind of life?
- Are you happy not to have a holiday during the busy season?
- Have you visited B&Bs to see what works and what doesn't?
- What about licences you'll need to run a B&B and serve food?
- Have you considered all that's involved in doing up a property and starting a business at the same time?

Fishing villages can be relaxing, sleepy environments, but in summer the tourists tend to take over.

The cons of living by the sea

At the coast you will be more aware of the seasons than anywhere else in the country. At various times of the year, this means picturesque places clogged with tourists and busy coastal roads. Then there's the serious risk of flooding in some coastal areas. Not to mention the fact that many of our seaside resorts are in serious need of regeneration.

The tourist invasion

Many coastal resorts have become desirable tourist destinations and are now expensive places in which to buy property. That doesn't mean that there aren't still opportunities to build an affordable life on the coast, just that you'll need to juggle your priorities with your budget. I remember meeting a lovely guy who was a keen fisherman. He had always wanted to live by water and pursue his hobby, but a lakeside

property had always been too expensive. However, he eventually found a beautiful new home and all he needed within his budget – the compromise was that to go fishing he had to drive through stunning countryside for about an hour to reach a lake. Not bad as far as compromises go!

Find out if the place you've set your heart on is a tourist haven and decide whether this will bother you or be great for your business. If you choose a popular spot, don't expect to have the place to yourself all year round. Ask yourself if you're happy to share your local town, beach and favourite haunts with the holidaymakers? If you're not, then look for somewhere less busy. Research your area carefully, both online and in person.

Don't rely on fond memories of an area before you start your search – our coastline changes rapidly. Many traditional resorts of the

St Ives
A B&B With a Difference

Andrea Carr and Peter Williams were planning an exciting new business venture and a new life by the sea when I first met them in 2004. They were selling an organic café in London to create a stylish, organic B&B in part of a disused hotel in the Cornish resort of St Ives. They had discovered the property on a weekend break and it was love at first sight for both of them. With the help of another investor and a huge loan, they bought the building for £750,000.

Andrea and Peter planned to split the property into three five-bedroom houses – one would belong to the other investor, one would be transformed into a five-bedroom luxury home which they would sell on, and the corner house would become Andrea and Peter's own home and B&B.

St Ives is a busy tourist town with loads of B&Bs, but Andrea, a set designer, and Peter, an organic baker, had plans to make 'The Organic Panda' stand out from the competition as organic and stylish. The property, however, needed a lot of work before it could be called either of those things.

The entire building needed a complete rewiring and re-plumbing, and all the walls needed to come down. It was a labyrinth of rat-infested rooms and a rotting extension. Once the whole place had been divided up into the three separate properties, Peter and Andrea would be able to do up the middle house to sell on before working on the B&B. This may sound counter-intuitive – surely it's best to get the B&B finished and get the money coming in first – but Peter and Andrea knew that the sale of the middle house would leave them with a manageable mortgage and a B&B up and running in time for Easter.

Meanwhile, they had a debt of over a million pounds. As this was a commercial development they were able to borrow 70 per cent of the money to buy the hotel, and then had to borrow again to fund the remaining 30 per cent. Because they'd borrowed so much, their priority was to finish the middle house first and fast – in just seven weeks. This would be worth about £425,000, making a good dent in their loan and relieving some of the pressure.

The old Dunmar Hotel, before its transformation into the Organic Panda Bed and Breakfast.

Peter, Andrea and George. In a town full of B&Bs, the Organic Panda had to stand out.

The long-term plan for Peter was to regain the quality of life he'd lost in London through working 6 days a week and 12–14 hours a day. Even though the Bed and Breakfast would be a seven-days-a-week job, the amount of actual work would be much less and he would be able to enjoy a different quality of life. Andrea was an equally important part of the project. Despite being based 300 miles away in London, she was in charge of design on the project. Working together, after seven years as a couple, was all part of their plan for a new seaside existence.

The build was slow, not always smooth, and put them under extreme financial pressure. By the end of the work to the B&B they had no bookings for the season ahead because they hadn't had the time to get anything set up. It took a further 11 months for them to break even. It was a long haul but when the guest rooms were finished they looked fantastic, as did Peter and Andrea's own living quarters. Andrea had focused on the gallery in the dining room and Peter's organic food was amazing. It was no wonder the business was proving popular.

Peter and Andrea underestimated the amount of work to do, and they faced constant financial worries.

Andrea says that they've experienced their share of Fawlty Towers moments along the way, for example when she was repairing a knob on a door while Peter had to keep the guests entertained downstairs until she sailed by to give the thumbs up behind their backs!

Despite these hiccups, Peter and Andrea are revelling in their new business roles, and, above all, loving their new life by the sea.

There's more on their project on page 145.

The finished kitchen looked superb. It had to be right because of the B&B's focus on food.

The dining room, where guests would enjoy Peter's superb organic meals.

The world of watersports opens up to you when you move to the sea.

1950s and '60s, such as Whitstable, for example, have become very fashionable over the last few years and are attracting a greater number of younger visitors, boutique hotels and busy eateries.

Of course there are options in between the bustle of somewhere like Brighton, with its volleyball, buskers, market stalls, packed-out beachside bars and cafes, and the deserted beaches of North Norfolk, for example. The important thing is to go and take a look, and see if the place works for you.

Busy coastal roads

In the summer season, you could find that the coastal roads you depend on for the running of your daily routine reach gridlock when the tourists swamp the beaches. Are you happy to be patient, join the queue or find an alternative, longer but quieter route? How will you feel when it takes twice the time to do the most basic chores or when hit by the pollution that comes from the build-up of summer traffic? And what about in winter, when the roads may be quieter but the wind carries up grit from the beach to slow down your journey?

Risk of flooding

If you choose to live by water, expect your home to be susceptible to damp. There are certain parts of the country where homes are prone to flooding – such as parts of Norfolk, Somerset and Sussex. It can be almost impossible to sell on a house that's in a 'flood zone' or has a history of flooding, and I don't need to tell you the kind of heartache such a home will potentially bring you. Then there's the effect on your annual home insurance premium when your property will be classed as high risk.

Be flood aware by looking out for wells in cellars in the properties you're considering. Find out the full history of the area from the local authority and check your solicitor's land search notes. Don't rely on estate agents giving you the full details and history of a home, they might not have all of the facts, or want to part with them.

Seaside towns in need of regeneration

Some of our seaside towns are pretty run-down. These areas may tempt you with opportunities for cheap property, but before you commit do your homework. Find out all you can about an area and pay a visit – it might be neglected and in decline, with a lack of amenities and a high crime rate. If so, you can't just cocoon

> It doesn't get much better than a stroll along the beach to wind down at the end of the day.

yourself up in your dream home while you wait for the area to become 'up and coming'.

Places such as Hastings and Margate are still cheap and have been said to be 'up and coming' for over 20 years. So far, nothing has changed. The transformation of an area tends to take far longer in seaside towns than it does in major towns or cities, and in the meantime, you'll be miserable. So live for today, not for how things might be in 10–20 years' time.

Despite these few potential downsides to building a new life by the sea, coastal living can offer a healthy, relaxing and exhilarating outdoor lifestyle. But if it's not for you, turn to the next chapter, to read about living in the wilds...

Seaside towns can be bleak in winter. Be sure you are happy with your new location all year round.

THE CONS

⌃ Tourist overload – will you cope?
⌃ Congested coastal roads in the tourist months
⌃ Flood risk, with knock-on effects on your home insurance
⌃ Run-down coastal towns – don't assume these deprived communities will change overnight

Build a New Life in the Wilds

Throughout history the wilderness has been seen as an evil, barren place. The remote corners of our British landscape have always been steeped in sometimes frightening myths and legends – a hundred reasons not to visit, let alone set up home there. But times have changed. I recently read a report in *The Guardian* newspaper which stated that between 2003 and 2004, 105,000 people moved to England's most rural areas in search of a lifestyle of fresh air, better schools and less crime – 105,000 people is the population of a good-sized town. The filming of *Build A New Life* has made me absolutely see the appeal of seeking a peaceful existence in the Great British countryside today.

The series took me to some fantastically remote corners of Britain, such as an enchanted wood by a lake in deepest Norfolk and an area of natural beauty in the Northern Pennines, as well as the countryside of County Limerick in Ireland; and even further afield to some isolated locations – in France and Croatia. It was truly inspiring to see the families featured in the show carve out a new life where they could really get away from an urban existence, enjoy dramatic views, nature and wide open spaces. But I also realised that it's not the right lifestyle for everyone. Living in the wilds is an extreme life choice. One that needs careful consideration. This chapter will help you to weigh up the pros and the cons of living an isolated existence in the Great British countryside.

The pros of living in the wilds

It's a romantic dream – an elemental existence where you truly are at one with nature and the

Not a single person, car, or other building in sight – a home set in the beautiful British wilderness.

If this is the sort of view you want, then up sticks to one of Britain's most remote corners.

city lifestyle seems a million miles away. You may be captivated by the idea of living a self-sufficient existence, growing your own food and keeping your own animals, or you are simply drawn to the calmness and utter quietness of a life that enables you to commune with yourself rather than with others.

Romance, peace and tranquillity

I've heard many people say that living in the wilds is the only way to really pursue the dream of living in the countryside today in its purest sense. They're referring to the romantic dream we have of a property that's miles from anywhere and closer to nature than neighbours – a dream of being able to see hills roll from our front door and hear nothing but birdsong and sheep in the morning. It's the idea of finding a unique piece of British heritage in the most romantic setting, that you don't need to share with anyone and that you can call home. It's the dream of living in an idyllic location of

natural beauty where your kids are able to play safely out in the fields until dusk, discovering wildlife. And where you can watch them from your living room as you look at the big sky and the weather change over your magnificent view.

It's knowing that to reach civilisation, or for it to reach you, takes a real effort. That a neighbour, family member or friend is not going to just pop round without prior warning and disrupt your day. That you won't be woken up at night because someone throws a party or returns home noisily after a few drinks.

This is a dream of tranquillity. Of getting away from it all and enjoying your own company, nature and absolute peace. Some people want to give up urban living completely to fund a new life in the wilds – such as Margaret and Paul on the Isle of Seil (see page 34). Equally, this could be a dream you come home to after the daily grind of a job in the city – the ultimate retreat – if you're sure that the travel is worth the rewards of complete peace.

Norfolk
An Eccentric Dream

'I can't say its everyone's dream but it certainly is mine ... to get away from the rat race,' said David Forster, one of the Great British adventurers from the series, in the original, wonderfully eccentric sense of the word.

David was a refrigeration engineer on 24-hour call from the family business he runs with his wife, Jenny. They lived with their two teenage sons, Steven and Freddy, in a small semi on one of Lowestoft's busiest roads. But David was also a fantastically ingenious inventor; his homemade car was one of his imaginative

creations, while another was a secret tunnel leading to a hydraulic platform, designed to make an organist miraculously appear on the stage of a tiny theatre! When I met him, the intrepid 47-year-old was about to embark on his biggest challenge yet – the renovation of an 85-ft disused water tower hidden in tall woodland in deepest Norfolk. David's dream of a new life in a magical tower, surrounded by natural beauty and away from the stresses and strains of modern life, was one of the most poetic visions I'd ever come across.

Every now and then a very special project comes along and this was one of them. The tower was a hidden gem, the setting magnificent and the atmosphere magical. It was the perfect retreat. 'The appeal is the quietness of it, the fact that you've got wildlife – it's amazing to see the deer with their antlers.' David told me. 'Sometimes when I come up here and I've had a very stressful day, I can sit ... and it's wonderful. You can just see the bees and the birds and the squirrels come up.'

But the reality of this project was that it would take David an enormous amount of work to convert a huge industrial building into a family home while working 16-hour days at his normal job.

The disused tower was never intended to be lived in. It had no plumbing, electrics or even a staircase. You could only get up it by climbing a ladder and the windows were tiny slits. It was built over 100 years ago, to provide running water for a grand house nearby. At the top is a magnificent room with 360-degree views across the Norfolk countryside. It has beautiful windows so that the estate gamekeepers could keep a look out for poachers. I think it's fantastic

It's not where everyone would choose to live, but then not everyone is David Forster ... unique.

The dramatic view as you look up into the main roof structure of the water tower.

that the Victorians decided to design a functional, utilitarian building such as an industrial water tower in the style of a picturesque romantic folly.

David bought the tower with an £85,000 loan from his mother and hoped to carry out the conversion for £30,000, which he'd taken from savings and the family business.

David had very ambitious plans for the tower for so little money. The roof would be stripped, insulated and re-tiled, new Velux windows added and solar power rods fitted to provide green energy. Underneath the roof, in the light and airy top room, which would become the sitting room, the stunning beamed ceiling and the windows would be preserved. Further down the tower, the two existing floors would be converted into bedrooms with bathrooms. David would add two new floors to create a third bedroom and a kitchen. On every floor he would have to punch in more windows to let in more light. The whole building would be joined by a handmade, 60-ft spiral staircase. At its base, David wanted a glass dining table to hover above the 40-ft-deep well shaft – to make a stunning feature. And in pursuit of his magical dream, he wanted to add an element of fairytale to his handmade staircase – tiny leaded cupboards containing a small book behind one, a glass behind another... 'as if Alice in Wonderland was falling down the stairs,' he told me. He was literally engineering romance into his design.

Work began on the tower that October. Because of the tiny budget, David had to do a lot himself, but for the big structural jobs he enlisted the help of a local builder. Before work could begin inside, they had to waterproof the tower, starting with the roof.

George and David halfway up the water tower, as the project begins to take shape.

The water tower viewed from the air, a romantic building set in complete isolation.

It was an awkward and dangerous job – hauling supplies 85 ft up the outside of the tower by pulleys, and clambering up ladders in order to strip off the roof tiles, insulate the roof, install the solar heating system and re-tile it. Over a quarter of the budget was spent and they aimed to get the roof watertight before the winter set in, but working at such high altitudes meant they were exposed to strong winds. Progress was slow and eventually the weather stopped work.

But nothing was going to stop David. He climbed up the outside of the water tower without a safety harness (which was a terrible idea) so that he could take down the weather vane perched on top of the tower to restore it. It bore the initials GC, after George Causden, the wealthy American stockbroker who had the water tower built to service his property.

David was also obsessed with clearing out the 45-ft-deep fresh water well. As befitted his truly unorthodox style, he bought an oxygen tank last used in the 1970s out of retirement to do the job! He spent more time working down the well than on the rest of the building, despite the fact he was responsible for rewiring the tower, putting in the plumbing and all of the internal work.

By my second visit, David was still focused on the romantic, eccentric pursuits of restoring the weather vane and clearing out the well. I helped out, but personally I'd have left all of those pieces of history down the well and got on with the build. Three months later, when I visited again, the well was completely clear and David had restored the vane, which he'd reinstated and then installed a time capsule, essentially putting the finishing touches on a job he'd barely begun!

I knew that David could only devote the hours after work and at the weekends to the build and I started to become very concerned that the tower would become David's long-term hobby, rather than a serious build with an equally serious deadline. His family seemed to feel the same. Jenny confided to me that 'some of David's ideas come to fruition and some of them don't', referring to an impromptu loft conversion that was never completed, and the time he attempted to dig his own cellar. I knew that David was impulsive, but he was also a talented engineer. And he intended to give something to his beloved wife who had 'been putting up with my quirky ideas and tantrums over the last 25 years' by finishing the tower.

When your ambition is so great, the challenge is always so great too. I really hoped that he'd finish the building and get the fairytale ending that he and his family deserved.

Contemplating the considerable amount of work still to do on the project...

When you live in the wilds your nearest neighbours might well be animals rather than people.

Isolation and solitude

Some people crave a solitary existence. They yearn for a home that's not just a very personal space, but a true escape from the rest of the world – somewhere to seek solitude, be alone with their family or other loved ones, or to commune with nature. They want the reassuringly constant sense of silence that's only ever broken by wildlife and an uninterrupted view that's dominated by nature and the weather. They speak of literally seeing and smelling the change in seasons and they notice when it's time for lambing, wildflowers or foraging. They enjoy painting, writing, walking or fishing in their free time.

The wonderful thing about building a new life in a remote part of the country is that the property available there is still relatively cheap in comparison to that in more popular, built-up areas. So while a family can often minimise their debt and buy a more spacious property, one parent can sometimes afford to work less than before, or maybe give up work altogether. It really does transform family life. I've seen many families brought closer together in this way. They're simply able to spend much more quality time with each other.

For others, a fantastic time for couples to build a new life in the wilds is when the children have flown from the family nest – as was the case with Terry and Marylin from the series. With their new-found freedom, they are then able to create something special and unique just for themselves, giving them a wonderful life together, as well as a fantastic home for children and grandchildren to visit.

Hexham
Against the Elements

Terry Flynn and Marylin Flemming wanted to create a peaceful home. In their early fifties, they'd been together for five years and both had families from previous marriages. Holding on to their day jobs as construction manager and accountant, they wanted to build themselves the perfect retreat and somewhere large enough for their grandchildren to stay.

Marylin sold her terraced house in Whitley Bay on the outskirts of Newcastle and for just £105,000 she and Terry bought themselves two dilapidated farmhouses in need of serious love and attention. They took out a mortgage of £105,000 for the renovation.

'It's something that I've always wanted to do, all of my life,' Terry told me. 'It's going to be something else; I know it's a bit of a wreck at the moment, but it's got a lot of character and it's the area as well, I fell in love with it immediately.'

Their new, completely isolated home is one that they worked incredibly hard to bring to life, literally building the dream

themselves, brick by brick. Their property was miles from anywhere, on the harsh, exposed landscape of the northern Pennines. But despite the extreme weather lashing at their build and the fact that they lived in a tiny caravan on site, this unbelievable couple, who were so in love, rebuilt the derelict cottages they'd bought together by hand. It's a truly inspirational story and an epic project. I remember getting a call from a mate of mine in Newcastle, an architectural technician called Dene King, the night the programme went out on Five. He rang to tell me how Marylin had put him to shame. He'd been watching the programme and to the side of his TV, out of the corner of his eye, he could also see his unfinished bathroom, which he'd half tiled. He'd been observing this tiny woman in her fifties use all of her guts, grit and determination to lift huge stone roof tiles and dig out a floor with a pickaxe, while he hadn't even finished off his bathroom in the same timescale of her build! He was completely embarrassed and

The rural superheroes! George with Terry and Marylin outside their run-down farmhouses.

Marylin was a woman whose spirit never waivered, even during the toughest times.

got out the tile cutter and grout the second the show finished.

Terry and Marylin's farmhouses dated back to the 16th century and had an incredible history. This type of structure, called an 'abate', is the oldest type of farm building in the area and is unique to the Scottish borders. An abate is a farmer's fortress – a fortified house that once served to house and protect people and animals from Scottish cattle rustlers. The entrance to the building was very low, just big enough to herd in the cattle and there were small windows to provide cross ventilation, rather than light. It's a crude and simple building with a rectangular floor plan, built out of huge chunks of stone. The farmer and his family would have lived on the first floor, above the cattle on the lower level. He would have accessed his entrance via a ladder or staircase, which he would have sometimes pulled in, to protect himself in his own home. The huge fortified walls are about 2½ ft thick. The building didn't just protect against thieves, but also protected against the forces of nature.

These buildings had been derelict for years when Marylin and Terry bought them, and being open to the harsh elements in their neglected state meant the roof and much of the interior had been destroyed. If left for much longer, they'd probably have fallen down, but Terry and Marylin had grand designs for them.

They planned to knock through the farmhouses to create a fantastic three-storey country home. On the top floor would be two bedrooms, perfect for when the family came to stay. The front door to the house would open onto the middle floor – Terry and Marylin's big master

These buildings were among the oldest type of farmhouses in Northumberland.

The landscape can be unforgiving, but Terry and Marylin loved everything about it.

bedroom with en-suite is on one side, a guest suite on the other. On the bottom floor, they envisioned a large utility room and a lounge, with spectacular views, leading into the heart of the house, a large traditional kitchen with a mezzanine family drawing room above. But the crumbling shells needed to be stripped back to their bare bones before building work could even begin. It was an enormous project.

Nonetheless, Terry and Marylin were determined to do all of the work themselves while holding down full-time jobs. Some people in their twenties wouldn't have taken on a project like this but they had 'guts and determination, hard work' to get them through it, in Marylin's words.

Terry took great care to ensure that everything he and Marylin did on the build was done properly, using traditional building methods. It was very admirable. They wanted their build to be of the highest quality, but it was a painstakingly slow process. It's easy to underestimate the amount of work involved to restore a building of this age. There's the joy of peeling back the layers of history as you go, but it takes special care and attention to restore, replace and renovate. Marylin and Terry showed patience and determination at each step of the way. When Marylin dug out the floor of the

> I drive up that road and it's all gone. I see the sheep and nothing else and I think "great". It's a hell of a feeling.
>
> Terry Flynn

building with a pickaxe, it took 25 [wo]man-hours just to finish a quarter of the job – shifting ten tons of rubble by hand.

This couple couldn't have picked a more remote location to call home, but although they loved the isolation, it did have a negative impact on their build. The only way to get to their house was down a long and narrow, winding dirt track that was

The building was certainly run-down, but it had a huge amount of charm and character.

Terry and Marylin even decided to rear alpacas on the land that came with their property.

impassable for delivery vehicles. All of the building supplies had therefore to be dropped at the top of the lane, leaving Terry and Marylin to load up and ferry any materials the rest of the way all by themselves. This was a constant and gruelling challenge, not least when the time came for them to concrete the floors. As the lorry was too big to get down their track, the couple had to make 15 tons of concrete themselves using two small cement mixers, wheel-barrowing it into the house and laying it by hand. To ensure the concrete didn't crack, they also had to get it all done in one day. With the help of Terry's sons, they worked until 10pm that night, in freezing conditions, determined to get the job done.

The Northern Pennines is a designated area of natural beauty, but the weather in this valley can be extreme. The blue skies and sunshine of summer can be short-lived and the winters are long and severe. During the build, Terry and Marylin were subjected to 90-mile-an-hour gale force winds and rain that lashed at their property, destroyed their temporary living room on site and threw their tiny caravan around like a boat at sea. Storms left big holes in their track, so as soon as the weather broke, the first job was to repair them, so that they could get materials to the house once again. It was only when they were faced with 5-ft snow drifts at their door that Marylin and Terry finally conceded defeat to Mother Nature. They stopped work, dug themselves out of their track and sought refuge in Whitley Bay.

But even during those toughest moments, Marylin and Terry saw all that was positive about their new life. 'We've got this mess ... but I've never been so happy in my life,' said Marylin when the storms wrecked their site.

'I drive up that road and it's all gone. I see the sheep and nothing else and I think "great". It's a hell of a feeling,' said Terry.

For more on Terry and Marylin's project see page 155.

Things begin to take shape inside the farmhouse as a makeshift bedroom forms.

Given the harshness of the location, getting the fire working was a priority.

George with Chris Palmer and his daughter Demelza in Ireland, experiencing what it's like to work the land.

The good life, self-sufficiency and ecology

For those brave enough to do it, living in a remote setting can be an opportunity to get back to nature, go green and live 'the good life'. It's still possible to buy a property with enough land to keep livestock, grow your own vegetables and provide for yourself in rural parts of Britain.

Some of the families featured in *Build A New Life* went one step further and decided to radically cut their costs by living off the land itself – such as Chris and Rebecca in Ireland (see page 62).

Your own piece of British landscape

There's nothing better than letting the kids run around outside in their very own piece of

You can keep the kids happy for hours by adding a paddling pool or set of swings.

THE **PROS OF** LIFE IN THE WILDS

- Romance, peace and tranquillity – a stress-free environment
- Isolation and solitude – no-one around for miles
- A sense of being at one with Mother Nature
- Owning your own piece of land
- Growing your own crops and rearing your own chickens, cows and sheep

protected land. It gives you the freedom to get on with the gardening, host a barbecue and cut costs during the summer holidays, and you can keep the kids happy for hours by adding a paddling pool or some swings. Giving the kids a mini park is cheap and healthy entertainment. There's no need to drive to a theme park or fair when your fun is there on your doorstep.

I remember David Palfrey in Wales (see page 23) selling off a plot of his land to raise money for his build during the series, but also transforming the garden that remained into a fantastic space for the family. He built a wonderful tree house and swings, which went down a treat with the kids. The result was that the whole family spent a great deal of their free time just hanging out in the garden. So many of the contributors from the series found that their kids spent so much more time playing outdoors than watching TV when they were able to muck about in an outdoor space far bigger than an urban garden. It transformed their family life.

The great thing about living in remote and isolated parts of the country is that even though you are downscaling and reducing your mortgage, it is still possible to end up with a significantly larger outdoor space than you had before. Many of those families featured in *Build*

A New Life moved from tiny gardens on suburban housing estates to owning 12 acres of land! Being able to potter around in your very own patch of British countryside, to have somewhere to relax in the open air or grow your own plants, shrubs or even vegetables, is an important part of the dream of building a new life.

It's a far cry from the supermarket trudge. Would you be prepared to grow your own food?

Ireland
A Self-Sufficient Lifestyle

Chris and Rebecca Palmer were fed up with their lives being ruled by the mortgage repayments. Rebecca had a high-pressured job that she hated and which was having an adverse effect on her health. The couple rarely saw each other.

So they sold their Yorkshire home and decided to move with their daughter to County Limerick in Ireland to live debt free.

It was an exceptionally brave dream – rather than having jobs, they would support themselves by becoming totally self-sufficient, growing their own food and keeping livestock. And if that wasn't challenge enough, they also had to turn a run-down house into a family home on a tiny budget with a tight deadline. But they were determined to make it work.

The property was stunning – a 19th-century farmhouse with incredible views across the valley and, crucially, 1½ acres of land. With a lot of hard work, they turned the rocky land into a smallholding and the interior into the home they'd always dreamed of.

Chris and Rebecca longed to live a very basic country life which would also allow them to reduce their overheads, their day-to-day costs and the price of their renovation project. The kitchen Rebecca longed for was wonderfully simple, consisting of a range (that would also heat the property) and a table. Simple tastes indoors and a bountiful smallholding outside amongst the lush green Irish countryside would allow the family to live a lifestyle rich in quality and time. The result would be like going back 100 years, to the Victorian era that Rebecca so admired.

'I cannot remember not wanting to own a really old house in the country and grow

The Palmer's dilapidated home needed a lot of work, and their budget was hardly generous...

The heart of the home, with its wonderful inglenook fireplace, in the process of renovation.

all of my own vegetables,' she said. And this was Chris's dream too. 'I've always wanted this sort of life, it's so peaceful, all you can hear is a tractor going up the lane on the other side of the valley.'

Chris and Rebecca pushed ahead with

their build and kept an admirable rein on their tiny budget. Overall, the build was slow-going, but through it all they managed to keep their brave vision alive, which was the most important thing, rather than packing up and returning to Yorkshire.

They were realistic about what they could achieve – both in terms of the speed of the build and the extent to which they could be self-sufficient. Rebecca realised that she would need to shop for certain essential items, such as Demelza's school uniform, but they would still make do and mend as much as possible.

I really admired their attempt at a slice of the good life.

For more on Chris and Rebecca's project see page 155.

Rearing chickens and other livestock was key to the Palmer's dream of a self-sufficient lifestyle.

The polytunnel up and running, where the family grew their own fruit and vegetables.

The cons of living in the wilds

Naturally, isolation has its downside. However much you try to be self-sufficient, there will still be times when you have to get around, and get hold of the supplies you need for day-to-day living. It can be difficult to know if complete quiet and solitude will suit you without experiencing the real thing. Those noisy neighbours *were* annoying, but hang on, somehow you're kind of missing them now…

Remote living – the flip side

As with any radically different lifestyle, it's one thing to think about spending a weekend or a holiday in a remote setting, but quite another to live there permanently. I've known people desperate to live this lifestyle say that when they finally moved out to a beautiful, idyllic setting and realised that they were REALLY on their own it was a very uncomfortable feeling.

So how would you feel?

If you're used to having neighbours around you and don't want to feel totally cut off from other people then you'll have to make a real effort to become part of the community. You might have to drive miles to do the most practical things that you take for granted in your current situation – visiting the local newsagents, buying fresh bread, getting to work or taking the kids to school. If you've found a property you'd like to buy, take a good look at what's around you. This might sound obvious, but there are often elements that can end up being of huge consequence to your lifestyle, that you might not initially consider.

Maybe you were really attracted by the idea of being near a farm, but the reality is the cockerels crowing at 4am and the constant smell of livestock and animal muck. You might find your local amenities are extremely limited. Your nearest village might be shut on Sundays or closed half-days on Wednesdays, for example. There will probably be fewer collections at your nearest postbox and fewer deliveries to your front door. As far as work is concerned, you may well find that working in your area of expertise is no longer feasible (see Chapter 9 for more on how to integrate your work with your move).

In general, my advice is always to road-test your new lifestyle before you decide to jump in with both feet and commit to buying a property (one of the most expensive things we ever do). I strongly suggest, therefore, that you rent a home in the area first. Stay there a month or so and get a feel for what life there is really like, day to day. Hopefully your stay in the wilds will confirm that this is the dream for you.

One thing is for sure, however, you won't get far without your car.

Being dependent on your car

Despite first appearances, living in a remote setting isn't always the environmentally friendly dream we like to think it is. The reality is that the more isolated your new location, the more you'll need to use your car to get around. A trip to the local shop to get some milk and the morning papers might be 20 miles away and public transport might only go through the nearest town or village. You might have romantic ideas of riding to work or the local village shops and sending your kids off to

> Always road-test your new lifestyle before you decide to jump in with both feet… .

THE CONS

- Loneliness and isolation
- Limited amenities
- Unable to do your normal job
- Utter dependency on your car
- Being at the mercy of the weather
- The land around you may not be yours

school on their bikes past the open fields, but what will happen in winter when the roads are wet, muddy and dark?

If you're a parent then you are likely to spend far more time in your car for your kids. As 'Mum- or Dad-cabs', you'll find yourself ferrying them around to friends' houses, after-school activities and to take part in what's on offer in local towns, when the countryside loses its appeal. The view from your car window is likely to be more pleasant than you're used to, but the roads, although quieter, can be far slower. You'll need to get used to being patient, planning trips so that you pick up all you need in one journey and measuring your routes in terms of time, rather than distance.

But what you must also do is factor in the cost of running your car in the wilds, especially in relation to renovating or building your new home. Frank in Croatia (see page 67) found that he had to invest £28,000 on a 4x4 – this was simply the only vehicle that was tough enough to get him up the mountainside to his remote home. Paul and Margaret on the Isle of Seil (see page 34) told me that they ended up spending around £60 a week on fuel – three times the amount they were used to paying.

In addition, they found that when they had building materials delivered, it often cost them hundreds of pounds to get them transported to their island.

The weather

The more remote and exposed your location, the more impact the weather will have on your lifestyle in the wilds. The *Build A New Life* contributors who lived in the more isolated settings (such as the far reaches of Scotland and Northumberland), felt the harsh nature of

In isolated landscapes you can be very exposed to the sometimes harsh British weather.

It may look like the perfect retreat, but remember, all land belongs to somebody.

the weather far more than I outlined in Chapter 1 (see page 28).

You'll also need to think carefully about how the weather will affect your renovation or build project. Landscapes with little shelter had our homeowners literally battling against the elements in the winter months as the driving rain beat down on their unfinished homes and snow stopped work. Be prepared for the weather to zap the very energy you're trying to put into your project. Think about starting work in the spring if possible, and always ensure your roof and windows are secure and watertight before the onset of winter. See Chapter 8 for more on how to timetable your build project in order to work with, rather than against, the weather.

Get off my land!

It's easy to think that if the countryside is on your doorstep, you can just step out there and use it. But this isn't always the case. You might find yourself with wonderful views of rolling hills but no access or right to them. Don't assume you can wander freely in the woodland at the end of your lane or let your children play in the open fields just because you happen to overlook them.

Have you thought about whether the land surrounding the property you've got your eye on is protected? If such land does not come as part of your new home that means it belongs to someone else. Bear in mind that your beautiful, romantic view could be transformed if the owner decides to sell it to a developer or change its use. It's vital that you find out about the designation of the land through your solicitor. They will check out the proposed searches in your area at the time that you want to buy to find out if any building or change of use is imminent. In the meantime, visit the local planning department and check the rural development plan for the area.

Building a new life overseas

Sometimes, when we can't bear the thought of a winter in the remote British countryside and we long for the sun, we think about alternative destinations in which to build a new life, locations that are further afield.

Maybe you're coming to the end of this section of the book and realising that neither a life in the British countryside, by our coastline nor in the wilds appeals to you. Don't panic, you're not alone and there are plenty of other options open to you.

Since the dawn of the British Empire and the adventures of Elizabethan explorers such as Sir Walter Raleigh, the British have always loved to flee our shores in search of a better life in other parts of Europe. And it's never been easier to invest in a property overseas, experience a different culture, a different way of life, a more temperate climate, and enjoy a radically different lifestyle.

France and Croatia
A New Life Abroad

Jason Park and Philippa Stevenson had only known each other for 11 months when they decided to trade a life under the grey skies of Aberdeen in Scotland for the warmer climate of the beautiful Loire Valley in France. They abandoned their high-powered, lucrative careers in the oil industry to transform the Chateau de Charly into a luxurious five-star B&B and a home for life.

It was a wonderfully romantic adventure and a beautiful property, but the reality of building their dream was tough – the couple were separated while the work was in progress and they set themselves an ambitious deadline of just seven months before opening to the public. Jason struggled to do all of the work himself on a property with the scale and grandeur of a British stately home, while Philippa continued to earn money working in Aberdeen to bankroll the project.

Jason lived alone in the huge chateau, speaking no French. Yet he managed to create two living rooms, which required new plumbing and electrics, as well as to decorate all the guests' rooms and en-suite bathrooms, all to five-star standard. Philippa visited at weekends, putting in hours of gruelling manual labour after spending a stressful week at work.

They also had to market their new business and couldn't afford to miss the tourist season. But this was a couple who had just got engaged, were excited at the prospect of possibly holding their wedding in the grounds of the chateau and dreamt of their future children playing in the grounds. Their project was a tough mental, physical and financial test, but they fought through it to realise their dream of a life together in a stunning historic building.

The couple met, fell in love and bought a chateau, all in the space of a few months.

The chateau was full of beautiful features, including this elegant staircase.

Frank and Alice Freestone made the biggest and bravest move of their lives on *Build A New Life* – setting up home and guest accommodation in a nature retreat in the middle of the mountain wilderness of Croatia. It was the ultimate dream for nature lovers wanting to live amongst wildlife in a remote setting. As Frank told me, 'every step you take the grasshoppers are jumping around you, the butterflies just come and land on you. We have about three varieties of deer roaming across the land, it's just fantastic. I feel like we belong there, I really do.'

Frank has always been passionate about wildlife and nature. As a boy he spent his time in the woods near to the Cambridge house he was born in and had lived in for 49 years. But Frank's surroundings had recently been transformed into a built-up estate. 'The countryside is forever creeping away from me,' he said. 'When I was a child there used to be trees everywhere.'

The couple's search for unspoilt nature took them to a remote part of Croatia, half an hour from the tourist hotspots on the Adriatic coast. They bought 13 acres of land and an old farmhouse, which they found on the Internet. It cost £56,000 and there wasn't another property in either direction for two miles. From savings and the sale of their Cambridgeshire home, they raised £165,000 to live on and with which to build the retreat until they were in a position to open the business. It sounded like a good sum of money, but the farmhouse had no electricity, gas or water and hadn't been inhabited since the Second

The couple's new location enabled them to get back to nature and enjoy a rural lifestyle.

World War. Frank, who was a builder by trade with 20 years' experience, could see the end product and wasn't daunted. With the help of his Croatian project manager, they constructed six log cabins in the woods at the back of the house, while the farmhouse was transformed into a lodge for themselves and their paying guests. It resulted in a truly spectacular new home and life in the wilderness.

Thirteen acres of National Park and an old farmhouse – not bad for a mere £56,000.

George with Frank and Alice. The Freestones immediately felt at home in their Croatian wilderness.

When a piece of British countryside becomes your garden, you know your dream has become reality.

Happiness!!

If you're still in any doubt whether to pursue your dream of Building a New Life, let's recap on the benefits that we've spelt out in this section of the book – these are just some of the advantages of the country life that I heard time and time again from the contributors to the series.

I can't think of one couple or family who didn't say, 'I can't believe how much this has changed my life. I wish we'd done this years ago!' Many were surprised at how the change in lifestyle had brought them closer together as a unit, like Paul and Tracy in Upwell, who found more quality time to spend as a family, while couples such as Marylin and Terry in Hexham and Paul and Margaret in Scotland were able to realise their dream of living together in total isolation, in a remote and beautiful setting.

Many people told me that for the first time they felt they were working to live, not living to work (and others managed to fulfil the dream of not working at all). People such as Glyn in Derby were finally able to adjust their life–work balance – reducing their stress and their working hours as they reduced their mortgage. While Rebecca and Chris in Ireland were a shining example of getting rid of life's financial worries altogether, when they began to live debt free. Gez and Laura in Worthing proved that you could live a sporty life by the sea and still pursue a career, while Andrea and Peter in St Ives built a new business into their plan for a new life, with their organic B&B.

Tracy in Upwell was finally able to give her horses a happy home, while David in Norfolk was able to realise his romantic dream of a wonderful tower in the woods. Countless other contributors developed new hobbies and passions, inspired by their new environments, new lease of life and the fact they had more time on their hands.

If you're harbouring a passion to Build a New Life and get out of the rat race, I hope that this section of the book has led you to the crucial question … what am I waiting for?

DESIGN
LAYOUT
MATERIALS
COSTS

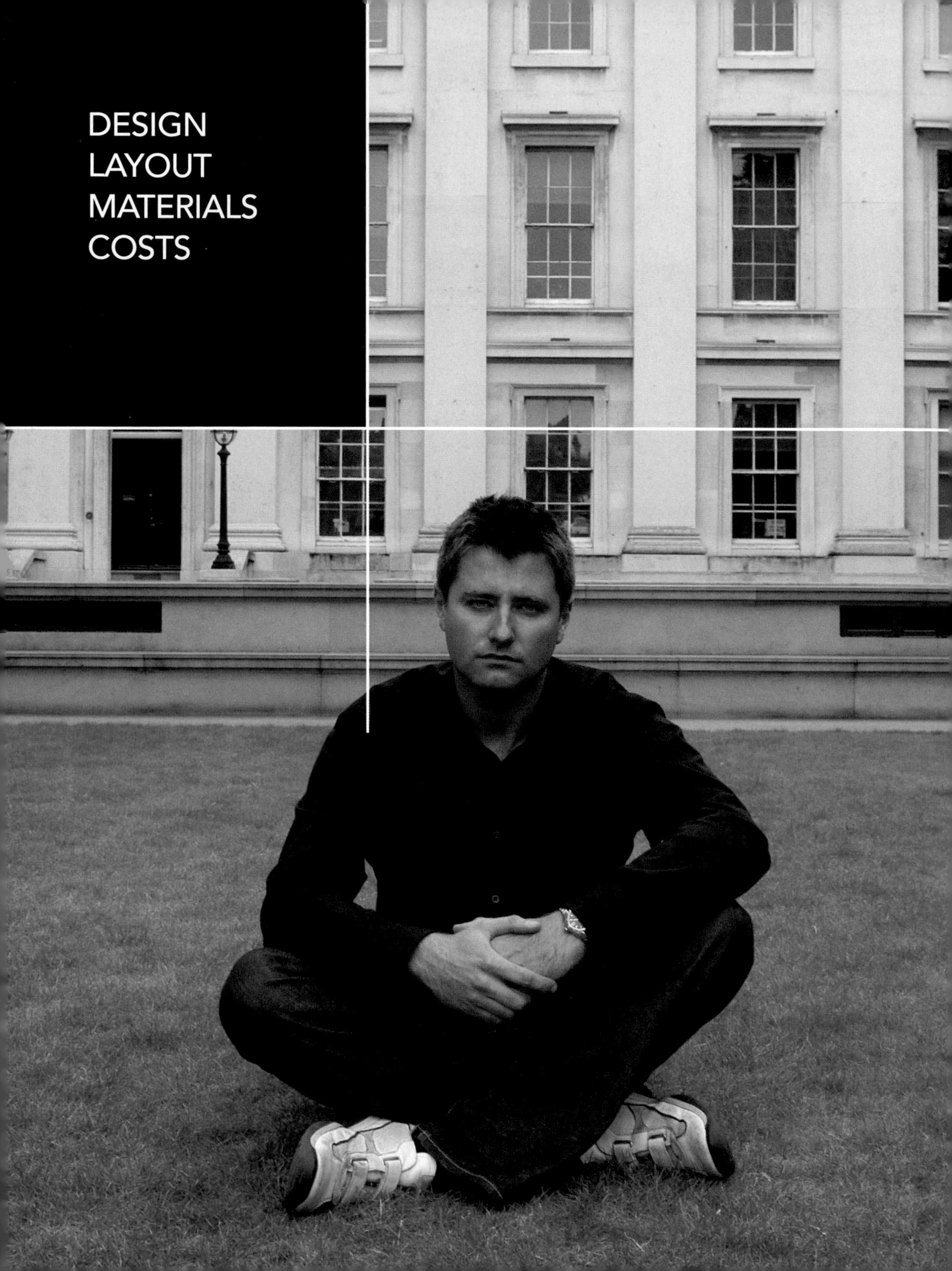

HOW TO DESIGN YOUR HOME

Now for the exciting part, where you can get creative and make your new home the space you really want it to be. This section of the book will help you focus on how to get the ideal layout for your lifestyle. Will you go for a contemporary or traditional layout, a renovation or a new build? I'll also guide you through ways to make your project as environmentally efficient as possible, and help you get to grips with budgetting and keeping costs to a minimum.

We've all driven past a beautiful old house that looks derelict and wondered what it might be like to cut back the overgrown brambles to reach the front door, replace its broken windows, repair its tired, creaking structure and breathe new life into that forgotten and neglected home to make it our own. This romantic notion is wonderful but it needs to be accompanied by serious thought if you're really going to successfully build a new life.

Section One of this book should have made you think long and hard about the new lifestyle you're trying to carve out for yourself and your family. By now you should know where in the country you'd ideally like to relocate to and why, and whether living in the country, by the sea or in the wilds is your dream. You should have spent some time in your shortlisted locations to see what it's like being there day to day, done some serious research into what these places offer, and found out about the kind of properties you might find there. Ultimately, you will have your eye on a new home and be seriously considering taking on a particular property to renovate and build your new life. But are you ready to take on a restoration project? Do you know what you'll do to the property to transform it into a wonderful home?

This section of the book will give you advice on how to decide what style to choose for your new home, how to plan a layout that really works for how you want to live, and how to translate all of your ideas into a concrete piece of design. There's a chapter dedicated to showing you how to choose and source the right building materials for your renovation project and how to find the right people to help you bring those materials to life. And crucially, the final chapter tells you how to keep all of this affordable. In short, this section of the book contains all the 'how to' information to help you visualise your dream so that you can start turning it into a reality. I'll guide you through what you need to do and how to avoid the common pitfalls so that you can be creative and get stuck in.

Whether you decide to opt for a cutting-edge modern interpretation, an authentic restoration, or decide to go green, this is your opportunity to strip back a building to its bare bones and put your mark on it. Whether you do this alone, get a main contractor to oversee the project, or employ a team of builders, you'll be transforming a forgotten wreck into a wonderful home that works just for you and your family. Or, you might even decide to build a brand new home from scratch. For many of you, a project of this scale will be a once-in-a-lifetime experience that will absolutely change your life forever.

Enjoy it!

CHAPTER FOUR

The Design Process

You've made the life-changing decision to relocate to the place of your dreams and change how you live for the better. As an architect, I passionately believe that the home you create will have a huge impact in helping you to achieve the lifestyle you're craving. It will be a major influence on your quality of life. This is your chance to design the home you've always dreamed of, rather than to buy something created for someone else's needs. It's time to generate new ideas and to utilise the very best ones you've gathered from magazines, TV shows, or visiting other people's houses. This chapter is devoted to focusing your mind to ensure that you get exactly what you want from your new home. You don't need to know every detail at this stage, but you do need to start setting out your main objectives. This is the fun part! Get creative, be inspired and be excited about making your mark on a property.

Your unique lifestyle

We all live differently and we all have our own unique lifestyle. This is your chance to design a home that will cater to yours. Your new home should make your everyday life run as smoothly as possible, reflect your personality, your tastes and respond to the needs of every member of your family. So the first step is to define what these needs are.

The best place to start thinking about how to design your new home is to look at your current home in some detail. This was a place that used to work for you, but doesn't anymore. Why not? A really useful exercise is to make a list of things that drive you crazy about your home. For example – the kids share a room, your kitchen is too small, there's nowhere to work from home or to relax outdoors. Think not just about the scale or the amount of rooms, but how what is in those spaces impacts on how you feel. Perhaps there is insufficient natural daylight, for example. And don't forget the practical elements, such as not having enough

The design phase is your chance to put your own creative touches to your new property.

Perhaps you crave the sanctuary of a lovely spacious bedroom hidden away at the top of the house.

storage or any grassed areas for your children to play on. By doing this, you've automatically created a list of why your home doesn't match your current lifestyle and you're already thinking about fixing those problems.

Now create a separate list. This should be a realistic wish list that reflects how you want to live now. Maybe you want the kitchen to be the heart of the home – a big room for family dinners and entertaining – and a large living room is not quite such a priority. Maybe you plan to work from home full time and want a beautiful, peaceful study. Maybe you plan on having more kids and will need an extra bedroom or two, or are sick of sharing one bathroom and crave the sanctuary of an en-suite. See the box on page 76 for some ideas.

Not only are you getting a feel for what your practical requirements are, you're also plotting your very own design brief. This is essential stuff and I'm sure you'll agree that it's not that hard to do. This initial stage is crucial because it will help you conceptualise your dreams on paper, which you can then use to brief an architect should you decide to employ one (the ideal scenario), or to help you with your own DIY project.

Architects use Room Data Sheets when they work for clients. These are A4 sheets of paper which note every single one of a client's requirements for a particular room (such as the colour walls they want, what the floor finish will be, how many plug sockets are needed, how much natural daylight they'd like, etc.). I hope that by the end of this section of the book you will be able to create these for yourself. It's a great exercise to help you understand how your new home should work for you.

WHAT'S **WRONG**   WHAT'S **NEEDED**

WHAT'S WRONG	WHAT'S NEEDED
⌃ Bathroom too small	⌃ More open-plan areas
⌃ Kids need a playroom	⌃ Large, private garden
⌃ No built-in storage	⌃ Family bathroom + en-suite
⌃ Office is in bedroom	⌃ Separate studio/office
⌃ Ground floor dark	⌃ Kitchen/diner opening
⌃ Garden is overlooked	to garden

Other people's homes

Sometimes it's not easy to decide on what might work best in terms of style, function and layout with everything that's on offer today. It can be difficult to choose between old and new, open plan or cellular spaces, colour, light and materials. What you need to do when it all seems overwhelming is focus on visualising your ideas.

My top tip is to collect magazines, pictures and brochures, tearing out things you like to make a clippings file or scrapbook. But don't stop there – see what you like about other people's homes. I love being an architect but I have to confess that one of the reasons I'm

A galleried landing can be a wonderful way to give your home a feeling of space and light.

obsessed with property is because I'm so nosey! I love having a look at how other people live and what works for them in their homes. And there's no better time to do this than when you're designing a new home – it really is one of the best ways of getting great ideas and trying out other people's lifestyles.

A good tip is to carry a small digital camera with you to snap any elements that you would like to add to your scrapbook. I actually go one step further (being a bit square) and carry a tape measure with me too. If I see a room I fall in love with, getting its dimensions helps me to work out why I'm so taken with it. Maybe it's the proportion of a high ceiling – so how high is that? Or maybe it's a wide space with a huge window which lets in a wonderful view – how large is that window? If I measure these elements, I can reference them when trying to design a room I know I'll love, especially if there are constraints, such as a small space that I want to make feel bigger by letting the outside in. Carrying a tape measure and a camera hasn't got me into trouble yet. People are usually flattered that I pay such attention to their home. We're a nation proud of our homes so we love it when people show an interest in where we live. And if that particular homeowner has renovated their property themselves, they'll understand your obsession.

Restoration or new build?

Almost all of the contributors from the series wanted to breathe new life into an old derelict building, resurrect a great piece of architecture and lovingly preserve it in all its glory. It's a romantic British dream that brings people great satisfaction and a wonderful sense of achievement. Some are drawn to a restoration project because they are passionate about a particular style of architecture or period in

Think about what it is that appeals to you in other people's homes when you visit.

history. Others love historical buildings because they believe that buildings are like characters who have their own story to tell. But renovations take a huge amount of determination and patience – and they're not always the most economical option.

As you've seen from the series, I'm passionate about restoring old buildings, but recently I found myself embarking on a new build. I bought a cottage built in the 1840s with wonderful views of the Dorset countryside. I planned to restore and extend it to create a spacious family home in the country. The cottage was in a seriously terrible state – it was damp, rat infested and needed an enormous amount of money spent on it. Eventually I had to admit that it was more economically viable to demolish the cottage and start from scratch than to work with the existing building to get the house that I really wanted.

This is not a new story. It's not unusual to peel back the layers of an old building to find huge structural problems lurking beneath, which can cost a vast amount to fix. These problems can't be anticipated or budgeted for.

If there's a focal point to a space, keep it that way and make the rest of the room work around it.

Sometimes, the constraints that are imposed upon you by the existing fabric of the building simply aren't worth battling with (like the impossibly uneven walls in Upwell, where it cost an absolute fortune to create a straight roof line – see page 19). In such cases, it just makes sense to start from scratch and build exactly what you want.

In addition, you can claim back VAT on any material costs of a new build, which will mean you'll get back 17.5 per cent of the amount you spend on materials. Unfortunately, this is a terribly biased law that doesn't apply to restoration projects. It was put into place at a time when the government was encouraging the building of new homes, but I feel that we should be able to claw the VAT back on restoration projects too. In other words, we should be encouraged to retain our historic buildings.

Traditional or modern?

This is essentially a question of taste, but also one of opinion. Do you believe that a traditional old building should be restored in a style that's close to its original structure, both inside and out? Or do you think that a period property can be enhanced by a contemporary interior or modern materials?

For most of us, this question isn't clear cut. While some people are keen to recreate an authentic historic home (like Jan in Derby, who spent all of her spare time driving across the Midlands in search of architectural salvage and antique materials – see page 16), rather more prefer to preserve some of the period charm and style while adding some modern design elements – especially technological ones – for a more eclectic take on the traditional. This can work, but only if it's done very well. If not, you

> Sometimes, it just makes sense to start from scratch and build exactly what you want.

run the risk of creating a scheme that looks like a standard developer home.

Creating a completely contemporary interior in a traditional property, as Matt and Emma did in their Lincolnshire barn (see page 21), can be a stunning solution. And it can still be sympathetic to the property if you're mindful of working the best period details into the design. The only marriage of styles that never seems to work, in my opinion, is a traditional style of interior in a modern building or new build. If you love a particular historical style

don't be tempted to try to insert it into a 20th-century building. It will always be a pastiche and will never work.

Eco design

I'm passionate about buildings, but I'm also aware that constructing or renovating them can be environmentally destructive.

Most people are just not aware of the impact that building has on the environment. We always think that cars are the worst everyday polluters, but that's not the case – the construction and running of buildings accounts for far more pollution if you look at the figures. A staggering 60 per cent of all global resources are used in the construction industry, whereas cars account for just 25 per cent. Maybe it's because we can actually see the pollution coming out of an exhaust pipe that we think of them as the worst offenders.

Fifty per cent of global water consumption is for sanitation and other building-related uses, while 60 per cent of global timber use is in the construction industry. In addition, 90 per cent of

TOP **TIPS** – ECO-FRIENDLY **DESIGN**

- Try to use local materials.
- Use timber from sustainable and renewable sources.
- Insulate your building to the highest standard.
- Use an efficient heating system.
- Use skylights and triple-glaze your windows.
- Avoid using air conditioning in buildings at all costs.
- Use tiled or wooden floors rather than carpets.
- Use green energy and renewable resources to generate power.

Tiled or wooden floors are in fact more environmentally sound than carpets.

all hardwoods forested across the world are for building use. This just can't go on. It's completely unsustainable and we have to change.

When constructing your own building, being eco-friendly is a challenge – not to mention one more thing to think of – but remember that you can make a significant impact on protecting the environment by doing some very simple things. Some ecological or locally sourced products are more expensive than others, but consider this against their effect on the environment and the money you can save on the long-term running costs of your

Try to source your building products and materials from the local area as far as possible.

home. There isn't room here to chart all the things you could do, but the box on page 79 gives many basic eco tips.

Throughout history, houses have been built from the materials that surround them. But today, many materials travel thousands of miles across the globe to be used in our homes, wasting a huge amount of energy and resources. When you're selecting materials, find out where they come from and try to source local products as far as you can. Not only will you be helping the environment, but also by building your home from the materials naturally found in your local area you'll be creating an architecturally more coherent building that will look and feel right. Always go for sustainable materials with a low environmental impact wherever you can.

Insulation is another area where you can save money while doing your bit to save the planet. Insulation is a relatively cheap way of efficiently storing the heat in your home. The money you spend on fitting your insulation will be recovered from what you'll save in heating bills. I always recommend that if you can afford to, go way beyond the insulation standards set out in building regulations.

Inefficient systems and boilers each produce an average of 3.6 tons of carbon dioxide emissions in their lifetime. Look at systems where the warm air that's generated during the day is efficiently stored to heat your home at night and use natural resources to generate power. You can easily collect rainwater to water your garden. And if you live in an exposed setting, install a micro wind turbine on your roof or on your land. Consider fitting solar panels too – you'll be amazed how well they can heat your water throughout the year.

Skylights provide fantastic amounts of natural light as well as 'stack ventilation' – letting any dirty smells or warm summer air rise up and escape in the way that chimneys do.

They naturally ventilate your home in the summer and retain the heat from the sun and central heating in the winter, provided you double- or triple-glaze your windows.

Contrary to popular belief, tiled or wooden floors are more environmentally sound than carpets. They have a longer life span and require less energy to make. Carpets also prevent the structure of your house from storing heat. Tiles, on the other hand, absorb heat during the day and slowly release it back into the room at night.

Finally, when it comes to eco-living, perhaps the most important thing is to simply avoid air-conditioning. In the UK we have a stable and comfortable climate. We don't need it!

These are just some of the ways you can use your location to your advantage. Try to be as excited about eco design choices as your regular decisions about your home. Do your research and don't ignore the fact that your

Skylights are a great eco solution as they provide both ventilation and natural light.

project will have an environmental impact. I know it's a cliché but if 'all' of us make our very own small effort to build and live ecologically it will make a massive difference to our planet.

DESIGN **CHECKLIST**

- ⌃ What are your basic requirements from a property? Remember to make two lists – see pages 74–76.
- ⌃ Make a scrapbook of design inspirations. Start buying interiors magazines, and carry a tape measure as well as a digital camera when you visit other people's houses.
- ⌃ Think carefully about whether a renovation project is the right option for you. Might there be some benefits to considering a new build?
- ⌃ Will you be attempting a traditional restoration or a contemporary fit-out of your new home?
- ⌃ To what extent will you go green? Remember to look into design solutions that are eco-friendly and source local, sustainable materials wherever you can.

CHAPTER FIVE

The Ideal Layout

So many people get caught up in the excitement of choosing the design details for their new home that they forget how important it is to first work out the perfect layout for their property. If you think of Le Corbusier's description of a home as 'a machine for living in', you can see how layout is fundamental to any home's success. When designing your layout you should be aiming to divide up the available space to provide a series of rooms that connect in a way that flows, ensure the scale of each room is appropriate to how you will use it, and ensure each room contains the fundamental elements which make it work for you practically, visually, poetically and emotionally.

This may sound complicated but it's not. This chapter will show you the simple tools and tips to help you get the layout, and therefore the home, you want.

The first and the most important piece of advice I can give you is that you make sure you get the layout of the property absolutely right before starting work on site. This is crucial. If you hold off and your contractors begin preparatory work in rooms that then change their location, you will lose time and money.

My second crucial tip is to keep your layout simple – it will be easier to build, will look better and will be more cost effective.

With these elements in mind, you'll be able to turn the inspirational ideas you formulated when visualising your home (see page 75) into a piece of beautiful design. Working on your layout is a fun and artistic process, but I would always recommend that you employ an architect to help you get it right. To get the very best from your architect, however, you'll need to have thought about the basic principles of layout yourself, and you must have a vision of how your new home needs to function for you. Later in this chapter I'll show you how to find an architect who will have a good understanding of your living requirements and your brief, and who is as passionate about your building as you are.

If your budget doesn't stretch to employing an architect I would advise that, at the very least, you get one on board during the early stages of the design process, to work on your proposed layout. Design is their skill and you'll be using your money wisely by tapping into this.

If you really can't employ an architect at all, you'll need to be equipped to design the complete layout yourself. It is possible and can be enjoyable too. I'll guide you through the process, using case studies from the series.

The layout to suit your lifestyle

In Chapter 4 I asked you to make two lists under the headings 'What's Wrong' and 'What's Needed'. The first listed all the things that drove you crazy about your current home, the second was your wishlist for your new property. Now's the time to dig out those lists.

Your lists should have helped you analyse your lifestyle. Now it's time to make the key

> You must have a vision of how your new home needs to function for you.

decisions about how many bedrooms you need your new home to provide, if you need an office or playroom, if you want an open plan kitchen/diner for entertaining and what you need from your outside space. Once you've found a property that has scope to offer you all this, or you decide to build a home from scratch that will meet those needs, you can focus more specifically on working the best parts of your derelict old building into your layout and/or making the most of the surrounding landscape in your design.

Gez and Laura's home in Worthing is a good example of how this can work. This young couple bought a plot of land right on the beach on which to build their modern home. They wanted a layout that would make the most of their sea views and their beach lifestyle. They designed a glass-fronted property that looked over the beach and minimised the amount of windows at the back of the property, which overlooked a busy road. They organised the layout so that the kitchen and dining room formed an open-plan space that opened onto the beach. They placed the living room on the first floor above the kitchen/diner and the master bedroom on the top floor, as far away from the entertaining area as possible, providing a quiet space with great views from the top of the

Always focus on making the most of your setting when planning the layout of your home.

house. In addition, they designed a triple-height void above the staircase to let in maximum natural light. It was a simple, sensible and successful layout that responded to the setting and their lifestyle.

Not all of the layouts from the series were quite so seamless, however, as Clare and Martin's experience shows (see page 84).

BASIC LAYOUT QUESTIONS

⌃ How many bedrooms do you need?
⌃ Do you need one large space for entertaining?
⌃ Do you need an office space?
⌃ Do you need more than one bathroom?
⌃ What sort of outside space will suit your family?

Devon
The Importance of Planning

Clare and Martin Williamson-Cary employed an architect to help them get the house they wanted in Devon – a comfortable home for the family to settle in for good.

The building consisted of two barns in an L-shape, with a lower section and upper section. At the back the barn was set into a bank, so it was quite dark inside. They positioned a small entrance hall in the lower barn leading to two bedrooms. Off to the side in the upper barn, to get over the lack of light, they designed a triple-height dining hall with a grand staircase and a galleried landing which looked fantastic. Most of the living space was situated on the upper floor, where there was a large open living room. At the far end of the first-floor living room, with no entrance of its own and with no access to the outside, was the kitchen. On the other side of the triple-height hallway, on the ground floor, was a master bedroom and an even bigger room where the bathroom was located.

This was the layout Clare wanted. She created her home on time and on budget, but I felt that a different solution could have improved the way the space functioned, and been more sympathetic to this lovely rural building. Locating the kitchen through the living room on the first floor meant that any shopping coming into the house had to go up the stairs and through the living room. The living room thus had to contain a lot of circulation routes. This, coupled with the necessary amount of windows, meant there were few walls in the room and placing furniture became tricky as a result.

Eventually, the couple bought an L-shaped sofa and placed its back to the fireplace, so the family could watch the TV, which, visually, was a compromise. Clare

The lack of walls in the open-plan living space meant the sofa was positioned facing away from the fireplace.

The new timber-framed windows went some way to getting over the problem of lack of light inside.

made a massive window a key feature of the bathroom – lovely in principle, but given it was on the ground floor, with people walking past, I wasn't convinced the room would ever feel private (despite their use of one-way glass), or if the size of this room represented the best use of space overall.

For more on Clare and Martin's project see page 122.

How to start designing the layout of your new home

You've got a list of criteria of what you need your new home to provide, you've thought about the lifestyle you want to lead, you know how many rooms you need and have seen examples of layouts from the series. Now, it's time to start designing the layout of your new home.

Sourcing and using the original drawings

If you're renovating an existing building, source the original drawings that were done for the property via the seller. (If you can't get hold of them, your surveyor will need to measure your property and do the drawings for you.) These will show you the proportions of the spaces that are there and will allow you to see whether the building has been adapted over the years.

Now you need to put together Room Data Sheets from all of the information you've gathered so far (see page 75) and see how the sheets work with the existing shell of the building.

Cut out shapes of paper with scaled-down versions of your rooms, put them on the original drawings in approximately the right order of layout and start moving them around. I know this sounds a bit play school but it's a very simple and interesting way to see where rooms can fit, where they just don't work and where you will need to rethink the proportion or elements that you had in mind and try fitting them again. It also highlights potential clashes with existing windows, doors and features such as fireplaces in the fabric of the old building.

It's at this point too that you need to decide whether to employ an architect or not. As I said earlier, I think anyone trying to change the

I would always recommend you employ the services of a good architect!

layout of a property and renovate it without an architect is mad, and if you're building a home from scratch, it's absolutely vital. Even if you decide to do as much as you can yourself, you will still need help from an architect to get permissions in place and to ensure that your plan complies with building and fire regulations. You can then decide whether you want to keep the architect on board to project-manage the build, or go it alone.

How to find a good architect

RIBA (Royal Institute of British Architects) provides a comprehensive service to people wanting to find an architect in the UK. You can read all about how this works at www.riba.org. Whether or not you use this service or seek out other recommendations, always try to find an architect who's local to the area. It just makes sense since they will understand local architecture and planning issues. If you then use them at the second stage of your project, they can visit the site easily and recommend local builders. When you've found a shortlist of architects whose work interests you or who have worked on similar projects to your own, go and see examples of what they've done and ask them for references. There's absolutely no reason why you shouldn't ask if you can speak to an architect's previous clients. You can then find out if they fulfilled their brief and responded well to both the clients' lifestyle needs and their property requirements.

Homes with traditional layouts tend to have a number of small, intimate rooms.

The big questions

Before you can complete the design of your new layout or employ an architect, you need to be absolutely certain of the style of home you're trying to create. Chapter 4 should have helped you on the road to this (see page 74). Here are some further thoughts on the main features of traditional and contemporary layouts, which should help you feel confident when making your final decision.

Traditional layouts

Living a traditional lifestyle in a beautiful old country building that's steeped in history is still very appealing to many people. Traditional living spaces are all about small-scale rooms and intimate spaces. Before central heating existed, rooms were designed to be cosy, with relatively small windows and fitted with fireplaces and doors to generate and contain the maximum amount of heat.

In traditional homes you would generally have a porch area, in which to kick off boots and shoes, leading into a formal entrance hall. Off to one side of the entrance hall there would be a drawing or living room at the front of the house, a separate dining room off to the other side and at the back of the property, the kitchen, sometimes with views over a garden and possibly leading to an outside or downstairs WC.

Upstairs, you were likely to find a simple layout of two or three bedrooms and a family bathroom. In Georgian and Victorian properties, the higher up you went in the house, the less ornate the décor – fireplaces, alcoves and decorative details were more simple in the top rooms as this was where the servants would be housed.

So how do you make a home that was designed many years ago work for you and your family today?

> There's absolutely no reason why you shouldn't ask if you can speak to an architect's previous clients.

Chris and Rebecca Palmer are a good example of a couple who made a simple, traditional layout work successfully for them (see page 62). Their 19th-century farmhouse in County Limerick had been derelict for nearly 40 years. It had character in abundance but needed a lot of work in order to restore it to its former glory.

The Palmers decided to keep the original structure and layout of the Irish farmhouse. They made the kitchen the heart of the home, with a traditional range cooker in the huge inglenook fireplace forming the centrepiece of the room. Off the kitchen was a scullery in which they could store fruit and vegetables from their own harvests. The living room had a simple rustic feel with exposed brickwork. Upstairs was a large family bathroom and two bedrooms – the master bedroom having spectacular views across the valley.

This simple, original layout worked perfectly for this family. They loved their open fires, the intimate rooms and spent a lot of time in the kitchen.

However, there's nothing to stop you respectfully adapting a traditional layout of a historic building to suit your own more contemporary lifestyle.

Lincolnshire
Traditional Layout, Contemporary Interior

We demand different things from our homes today than we did 100 years ago. Rather than cosy, intimate spaces, we yearn for larger, open-plan rooms full of natural light. This is especially true now that we can keep them warm with central heating. We tend to want more bathrooms and en-suites rather than the traditional downstairs WC and upstairs family bathroom. We also like a mix of public and private spaces. So how do you keep the spirit and character of an old building alive yet make it work as a luxurious modern home?

Emma and Matt Cupper's home (see page 21) is a perfect demonstration of this. As a former granary, their barn already contained some large spaces and beautiful brick arches surrounding vast windows. These were the qualities of the building they'd fallen in love with and they realised that if they sub-divided the big spaces they'd lose its unique character.

You enter the barn into an impressive double-height hallway and are guided upstairs by a solid oak staircase. On the

The light-filled, open-plan living space formed the centrepiece of the Cupper's new home.

first floor, a suspended walkway connects the two halves of the building. On one side is a bathroom and three bedrooms; on the other, a study and master bedroom with views across the countryside. I encouraged this layout so the adults would have some privacy in their master suite, and as an alternative to putting another floor above, which would have lost the sense of drama and light. On the ground floor is an open-plan kitchen flooded with light from two large doors. Beyond is the centrepiece of the house – an open-plan living/dining room.

This solution worked perfectly – Matt and Emma managed to incorporate the latest in modern design without destroying the original character of the building. The contemporary kitchen they inserted into the old building was a success because they got the balance right – they kept the exposed timber beams as a feature and laid a slate floor for some rugged texture against the new shiny surfaces. The kitchen provided an informal eating area for the family, while the living/dining room would be used to entertain guests.

Matt and Emma got the balance right by mixing traditional materials with modern touches.

kitchen

living area

bedroom 3

bathroom

en-suite

bedroom 2

bedroom 1

An example of a contemporary single-storey house plan, showing open-plan kitchen, dining and living areas, with two generous bedrooms and a smaller third bedroom/study. This is an efficient layout with few corridors and where all the rooms requiring drainage are adjacent to each other.

Efficient planning

One of the keys to designing a successful layout is to make the design work as efficiently as possible. This means minimising the amount of potential wasted space – where corridors, hallways and areas such as utility rooms might detract from the spaces you want to prioritise. Revisit your Room Data Sheets or visualise your set of rooms as a jigsaw that you need to fit inside the shell of the property ... Here are some golden rules on how to crack the puzzle.

The staircase – The position of the staircase is one of the most important elements to get right and it's worth spending lots of time on this. The staircase determines everything – the journey from the front door to the stairs and at what point the hallways, corridors and rooms will lead off from it. Think hard about whether the staircase should be a key feature in the property or if you should minimise how much space it takes up. Often, the simpler the design and the fewer the number of corridors, the better. In my

Place secondary rooms in the more awkward, unseen spaces in the house.

house in Dorset the ground floor of the property is open plan with the staircase positioned at the rear of the building. Up the stairs on the first floor a bathroom is straight ahead with a cluster of bedrooms around it, with no space lost to long corridors.

I love placing skylights above staircases – this bathes stairs in direct sunlight all day long and transforms the staircase into a feature. It's a very useful device for converting dark, traditional old buildings that wouldn't have had many windows in their original structure.

Light – This is crucial to designing an efficient layout. Think about where natural daylight will come into the building and how you'll want to use your rooms throughout the day. Most

people prefer an east-facing bedroom so that they can make the most of the morning sun. If there's a part of the building that's south-facing, this is a great potential position for the room in which you spend most daylight hours, such as a home office, as you'll get good natural light from dawn to dusk. However, north-facing spaces with soft light rather than direct sunlight can be equally useful, especially for artists and people who like reading or have a beautiful library to protect.

Secondary rooms – Place bathrooms, utility rooms and boiler rooms in the more awkward, unseen spaces in the house and in areas that don't get any natural light. This means they won't carve up your layout.

There are plenty of useful tricks you can use to make the most of these rooms (see page 94). This is particularly useful in old buildings where you might be struggling to position your key rooms around existing windows to keep a natural symmetry (see my tips on Alignment and Natural Light on pages 93, 95). The most efficient and eco-friendly solution in such situations is to position all of your first-floor bathrooms over your ground-floor kitchen and utility room so that drainage and waste can exit efficiently at one point. If you design all of your services at opposite ends of the property, you'll have to pay thousands of pounds to double up on your plumbing and it will put extra time onto your renovation schedule.

My final piece of advice is to open up your mind to different solutions. An open-plan kitchen/dining area can free up space in the house for other rooms and might mean this room opens onto the garden, for example. Look at all of the possible options and think about how certain layouts could free up other parts of the building before you decide on what the most efficient plan is.

The Isle of Seil
A Missed Opportunity

Paul and Margaret Drew planned to bring their tired tin church on the Isle of Seil back to life by re-designing the space to give them a dream home as well as an area they could rent out (see page 34).

The old vestry and altar area became a self-contained flat with its own private entrance, while Paul and Margaret's own home occupied the remaining three-quarters of the church. By adding a first floor to the building they created three bedrooms and a family bathroom. A galleried area looked down into the dining room, while a rectangular stained-glass window served to retain the church theme. Downstairs, the original church doors opened to a glass-walled hallway off which branched the kitchen, living and dining rooms. The large windows took in the spectacular views of the island.

Paul and Margaret had done a pretty good job of designing their new home, but I could see that a rethink of the design could make the layout work more efficiently and make the most of the available space.

The hallway they had created was tiny (about 3 ft x 4½ ft), and although they planned to use glass bricks in this space, it would still have felt claustrophobic. I wanted them to re-design the hall by reducing the size of the kitchen very slightly and thereby providing a more impressive entrance to the church.

Paul and Margaret designed themselves a separate living room and dining room. This was fine in principle, but both rooms were small in scale. I suggested they knock the rooms into one and fit folding or sliding doors. This would create a larger, airier space that was flexible and could still

The tin church looked impressive from the outside once the exterior work was complete.

The Drews managed to retain some of the church theme, but their main rooms were small.

Fitting larger double doors could have enhanced the sense of space in the dining room.

The couple designed an art deco glass wall to divide the kitchen from the hallway.

be divided to create two more private, intimate areas. They had also designed these rooms to be accessed through single doors. These didn't really align with the existing architecture of the building (the windows in particular) and seemed an arbitrary choice. I suggested they fit more dramatic double doors which would align with the windows and create a beautiful sight line as you approached them from the corridor.

Finally, the couple had designed a space they called their 'gallery'. This was a space over the first-floor dining room defined by a balustrade edge, which enabled you to look down over the dining room. I suggested they make this extend over the living room and take the whole area up to double-height space, lit by skylights in the roof. But Paul and Margaret didn't go for my plan.

In general, this couple's original layout featured too many cellular rooms that didn't open onto each other. By inserting lots of small rooms into the building they compromised on space and light and by not aligning the new elements they were left with a rather unnatural feel. I think, perhaps, Paul and Margaret were a little frightened to go for what I suggested. They were so embroiled in the design they'd created that they were unable to take a step back and make the big decision to change it all at a crucial point in the project.

Get drawing!

You might think this sounds a bit nerdy but, as an architect, I carry a tiny A5-sized sketchbook with me wherever I go. These books are full of drawings and ideas. It's where I work out every stage of every design, from planning the house to designing intricate details.

Sketching your ideas is a way of testing them out. Many people I talk to about this just say, 'I can't do that! No way, I can't draw'. Rubbish! If you can pick up a pencil and make markings on a sheet of paper then you can draw. Drawing helps you to visualise and understand your thoughts and tells you if they'll work. Whether it's on the back of a napkin in the pub or in a big sketchpad, you should draw all the possible solutions for a layout, even if you haven't sketched a thing since you were five.

I might draw the same bathroom six or seven times – thinking about where the light comes from, where the door should be, where I should put the bath, and so on. Only by drawing the possibilities can I really answer these questions. For this reason, I would also advise you never to go by your architect's first set of plans – you should be testing and pushing them by asking to see drawings of different solutions.

The important details

Once you've thought about the Big Questions of which sort of style to go for, you've decided on the basic scale of the rooms, considered the positioning of key elements and have a nice full sketchpad (!), you need to think about some of the more detailed, but no less important, aspects of layout.

Alignment

Alignment is a broad, general principle and one that sounds quite technical, but is simply concerned with respecting a building and its elements. Think of your property as an external

> Whether it's on the back of a napkin in the pub or in a big sketchpad, draw all the possible solutions for a layout.

skin with walls – if you put something alien inside that shell, something that doesn't respect the building, it will always jar and look strange. If you design a harmonious interior, on the other hand, you will have a wonderful conversion that will look like it was always meant to be that way.

The very worst examples of renovations that ignore the principles of alignment are often found in badly designed B&B's, and many people I know can vouch for my regular condemnation of B&B Britain! What gets me cross is the urge to carve up the interior of beautiful old buildings in order to squeeze in the maximum amount of bedrooms and bathrooms. Often the proportions of the space are wrecked, windows are put out of alignment, doors are forced into bad positions, fireplaces and other features are ripped out because they no longer fit, and long, dark corridors are put in their place.

Let buildings speak to you. Look at their original features, the focal points of their rooms, their proportions – they're like old characters with their own individual charm, quirky characteristics, good points and bad points. Think about how to keep hold of the pieces of history that have quality and how to align any additions with the

BAD PLAN

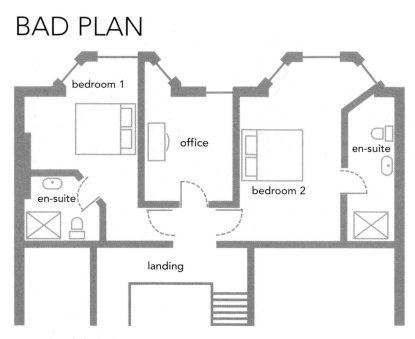

A poorly refurbished Victorian home. None of the new walls are aligned or balanced well with the existing architectural features. Instead, they divide up bay windows and the new en-suite bathrooms are awkwardly positioned, destroying the proportions of the rooms.

GOOD PLAN

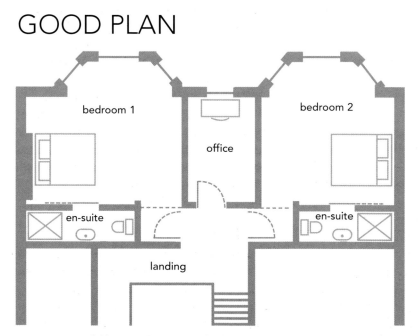

A more successful layout. The en-suite bathrooms and the office space are smaller, but far more efficient. The elegant bedrooms are aligned beautifully with the bay windows.

TOP **TIPS** – ALIGNMENT

- Keep focal points such as fireplaces central when dividing up a space.
- Avoid dividing up rooms with high ceilings to make two tall and thin spaces.
- Ensure you can still access each room easily.
- Ensure doors and windows are not awkwardly positioned.
- Consider transforming a small en-suite into a wet room.

existing building. For example, when you walk into an empty living room in an old property, what's usually left in the middle of the space is a fireplace with a chimney stack running up the centre. If you start cutting up the space without thinking, the room will become completely out of alignment – if you subdivided the room with stud walls to make a kitchen you may find the fireplace is no longer in the centre of the room. You'll lose the balance of the room, its focal point and its proportion, so it will never have the feel of the original.

In my house in London there is a large central window divided into three – and the room it's in is equally large. Lots of people have asked why I didn't divide the space into smaller rooms, so that there would be one bay of the window in one room and two in another. But if I had done this I would have completely lost the quality of the room and ruined the window that made the space feel so special.

I'm not saying that you can't change the layout of the space – of course you can – but the difference between creating a good and bad conversion is to do this with alignment in mind. What impact does a change of space in one room have on another – does it create an

awkward shape? (For example, if you cut a vast room with high ceilings into two you'll end up with two rooms that feel tall and thin.) Where will the windows be positioned? Can you still access the rooms easily? Finally, always look at whether the space you'll end up with after subdividing is really worth the effort. Will it leave you with an en-suite that never feels quite big enough, even with your scaled-down suite? Or can you transform this space into a great wet room?

Before you make your decisions, draw your plans and look at all of the options. If you get this wrong on paper you will get it wrong on the build. And you will destroy the character of the building that you're desperately trying to preserve. Of course, if you're hiring an architect they'll be able to guide you, but be mindful of alignment when you're checking their plans too.

Natural light

Many traditional old buildings weren't designed for us to live in – some were designed to house animals, others had commercial or agricultural uses – and contained only small openings or very few windows as a result. But this doesn't mean you should be restricted by the original blueprint for your new home.

Floor-to-ceiling windows always bring a sense of drama to a space.

Many of the contributors featured on the series transformed small, dark buildings into light and airy homes which brought the outside in by increasing the scale of the windows or by adding additional glazing in a way that was sympathetic to the architecture of the property.

A property designed to let in a lot of natural light will feel like a fresh, airy space and will naturally make us feel good. And remember that the light in a property changes its character and atmosphere as the day progresses – from the burst of early morning daylight to the warm glow of the setting sun. I don't think you can overestimate how much the presence of natural light can bring a building to life.

Windows also maximise or frame a view – whether it's across a valley, over lush green countryside or out to the cool blue of the sea – and windows can be used to increase the sense of space in a room by letting more of the outside in. Conversely, by excluding windows you can mask what you don't want to see.

Here's how some of the contributors approached the question of natural light:-

Matt and Emma Cupper preserved the full-length arched windows in their Lincolnshire granary with dramatic effect. Floor-to-ceiling windows are beautiful, especially if you have a great view – and they did. In Worthing, Gez and Laura had virtually the whole of the front of the house glazed, to make the most of the beautiful views to the sea and so that no further windows needed to be placed on the back of the house, which overlooked a busy road.

In Devon, Clare's property was buried into the ground at the rear, leaving her with a dark ground floor that seemed impossible to squeeze more windows into, because of the L-shape of the building. Eventually she fitted a huge skylight above her triple-height dining room – and then she played with the drama. She installed a fireplace next to the dining table, wrapped a staircase around both of these features and ran a balustrade around the top of the galleried dining area. It's a very dramatic, dynamic circulation space and a master stroke in terms of architecture and design. The skylight smothers the whole interior in direct light as it bounces off every wall and surface and brings the staircase to life. I also used very affordable Velux windows in my own house in Dorset to transform a dark, dingy stairwell (see page 160).

Making small rooms feel bigger

Windows and openings increase the sense of scale of a room. If you're struggling to cram four bedrooms into a building that can really only handle three, maybe you'll need to make one of these a single room. If you're then able to increase the opening of an existing window in that single room and so invite in views over the landscape, the room will feel much bigger than it really is.

Quite often, to maintain good alignment in a bedroom and create an en-suite, you need to make the en-suite a small room. This is the right solution. There are so many devices you can have recourse to in order to trick the eye into thinking a small bathroom is a good-sized space. Firstly, don't worry if the room doesn't contain any windows – if it's on the top floor of the building, install a skylight to bring in natural light and make the space feel bigger. Next, put in the biggest mirror you can – it looks wonderful if you can cover one complete wall. The mirrored space will give the illusion that the room is twice as big as it actually is, plus you'll see the reflections of the skylight and gain twice the light.

Don't be afraid to use the standard tricks of interior design. They might seem hackneyed, but they work. Paint small spaces as light a colour as possible – going for a dark colour will always make the space feel smaller and darker than it already is. Avoid cramming in large pieces of furniture but keep the pieces in

Using a mirror to give the illusion of space in a small room is a tried and tested trick of interior design.

proportion with the scale of the room – and limit the amount of things you choose to decorate it with. Clutter is a killer.

Finally, think about how spaces connect or flow with each other to give a greater sense of space. Knocking two small rooms into one open-plan area, leading the eye from one room to another, can create an enhanced sense of space, as can raising the height of a ceiling into the eaves.

If you're still in need of ideas for a spatially challenged room, why not visit a small inspirational building? One of my favourite buildings in London is the John Soane Museum. Soane was the absolute master of layout tricks. He transformed what would have been a tiny, dingy breakfast room in the heart of an old terraced house into truly magical space some 300 years ago. He did this by raising the height of the ceiling and putting a lantern in the top of it. Then in the four corners of the room he knocked through the openings and put in little panels of mirrored glass here, and did the same in the doors. This room is only

Consider storage, such as walk-in wardrobes, as an integral part of your layout.

approximately 6 ft by 7½ ft – just enough to get a table in – but it feels much larger because it blends into the other connecting spaces in the house and it bounces light around. I still use these tricks today, reinterpreting his principles in new ways.

Storage

Now that you're well on the way to designing the layout of your home, it's time to incorporate some storage. So many people fail to consider storage until right at the end of the layout process and then ruin the alignment of their rooms by adding in last-minute solutions or clumpy pieces of furniture. If you're really going to get the house you want, you need to consider storage as an integral part of each room's design.

I always recommend that you integrate storage as much as you can, so that it feels as though it's part of the building and looks as if it's meant to be there. Think about where you can place a cavity wall in a bedroom to fit in a built-in wardrobe, for example. And don't restrict your thinking to walls. If you buy an unusual property, get creative when incorporating the storage you need. For example, David designed 2-ft-deep cavities in the floor of his Norfolk water tower with lift-up lids to provide storage (see page 52). And in my Dorset bathroom we used an alcove in which to build a lovely, multi-functional piece of furniture which ran from floor to ceiling. You can buy some great ready-made solutions for tricky rooms – such as beds that fold down from walls or desks that fold away into a massive storage wall which you can conceal with paintings – so take advantage of what's out there.

If you're passionate about a certain piece of furniture that you treasure and want to reuse it, think about how it could be designed into your scheme, work successfully in the space and become a feature.

For a successful layout, consider sight lines and work to align your design with the existing architecture.

LAYOUT **CHECKLIST**

⋏ Always design the layout of your home before work starts on site.
⋏ Employ an architect to help you get the home you want.
⋏ Decide on a contemporary or traditional layout before you start.
⋏ Use Room Data Sheets to plan your layout.
⋏ Sketch your ideas and layouts so you can visualise whether or not they'll work and exhaust all the options.
⋏ Work to align your new design with the existing architecture.
⋏ Design your home so that the layout is efficient.
⋏ Remember that the position of your staircase is key.
⋏ Make the most of natural light.
⋏ Use tricks to make small rooms feel bigger.
⋏ Design storage as an integral part of your design.

Choosing Materials

Choosing the right building materials with which to construct your home is fundamental to its success. It will make a huge difference to the style and quality of your restoration or new build and will help determine how well the property functions.

If you're restoring an old building, it's crucial when choosing your materials that you respond to the history and style of the architecture as well as to the style of other local buildings in the area. Some properties cry out to be restored with traditional materials such as lime and timber. These buildings also demand quality. There's nothing sadder than seeing a beautiful old house that's had its timber-framed

windows replaced with UPVC, its roof patched up with mismatching man-made slate, or a new extension added in a cheap, jarring new brick stock. It's disrespectful to the unique piece of history that you, as the new owner, are now responsible for.

There are lots of wonderful modern materials and products on the market, as well as innovative building techniques, but it's important to use ones that are of as good a quality as you can afford and are right for the context in which you're building. Respect for location is also key – today so many new homes are constructed from the same products, irrespective of which part of the country they are in. From Dunkirk to

Slate is often used for roofing, but can work wonderfully as a decorative material too.

Devon, developers use fake roof tiles that have been flown hundreds of air miles from remote corners of the world just because they're cheap. Yet they're costly to the environment, aren't built to last and can't weather our climate. Natural, locally sourced materials are often more expensive, but they're produced to last and will add to the overall design of your home, plus they'll increase the value. A property in Dumfries that we featured on *Build A New Life* was constructed out of a fantastic red stone that's only found in that part of the country. It's a material that has a unique quality, can bear up against the extreme local climate and blends beautifully with the landscape. It will last hundreds of years, has a very low environmental impact and keeps the traditional architecture of that area alive.

When you've chosen the materials you want to use to restore an old building, a master craftsman can really help to bring them to life. Master craftsmen have a passion for restoring period properties, the knowledge to make the right choices both for your budget and the building, as well as the expertise to work on the property in accordance with the way it was originally constructed. And there are usually good reasons for their traditional methods. A craftsman can help you re-use the materials from the existing building, saving you money while you also do your bit for the environment. They are also fantastic sources of knowledge and can tell you where to find reclaimed materials from other period properties that you could also use.

This chapter is a starting point to choosing the right materials for your unique project. Basically, style, cost, quality, craftsmanship and environment are the five key factors to consider for each and every decision you make. But first, it's important to understand a little more about the key materials you'll come across and how to get the most out of them.

Using locally sourced materials, such as this lovely red Scottish stone, is always recommended.

Stone

Stone is a beautiful, natural material. It's versatile, tactile and no two pieces are ever the same. If you look around you, you'll see that stonework graces our rural landscapes as well as our towns and cities in great historic examples of British architecture. From the elegant curved sweep of the Georgian townhouses of The Royal Crescent in Bath to the humble stone-built cottages scattered throughout the countryside of England, Scotland and Wales, stone masonry has been used to create both theatrical building statements and solid, worker's homes throughout history. Today, there are still many natural stone quarries scattered around the country, so if you're lucky enough to buy a lovely old stone-built property, there's no excuse not to use stone to restore it.

My first tip would be to do some research on the stone that's been used in your new property – chances are it will be of local origin, which will allow you to find both craftsmen and quarries in your area. My second tip is to hunt for old buildings built of the same stone and around the same period as your own that are being pulled down. This is ideal if you're looking to seamlessly patch up missing or decayed pieces of your property. Finally, I would always recommend that you employ a master craftsman to build or repair any stonework. It's a highly skilled job that requires a knowledge of the material, the traditional building techniques and the masonry mortars, not to mention which type of stone to use where. Stonework can chip, flake, become dirty, or fall into disrepair over time, and although water damage or weathering is one culprit, poor repairs are undoubtedly another.

There's simply not room here to explore all the types of stone and their uses, but to inspire you to do your own research, here are two examples from the series where wonderful stone buildings were restored to their former glory.

When restoring their home in Wales (see page 23), Rebecca and David Palfrey sourced

> # Style, cost, quality, craftsmanship and environment are the five key factors.

a beautiful green stone from a local quarry. It's a material that very much defines the local area – almost every building surrounding them was made out of this stuff. It's a solid Welsh stone that creates 3- to 4-ft thick walls and is laid by master craftsmen in a traditional way, following a technique similar to dry-stone walling. The stone is perfect for its environment – both visually and practically – and so thick that there's no need for insulation at all, which makes it environmentally friendly too. So often today we use a thin facing of tile on the front of an exterior wall, build it up with concrete behind, then add a layer of insulation and plaster on top to get a smooth finish for the interior – a bitty and inefficient sandwich! These thick Welsh walls instantly protect against the weather, define the strong, robust look of the local architecture and age better with time.

In Hexham, Terry and Marylin stumbled across a unique and unusual property when they found their stone house (see page 56). It's one of the few I've seen that's completely constructed from stone – from floor to roof – and has stayed largely intact. Well, almost! Adjoining the main house was a 'bastle' (a fortified barn – half barn, half castle – hence 'bastle'), which was originally built to house the animals that worked the land. This part of the

This beautiful green Welsh stone is expertly laid by master craftsmen and defines the local area.

building is incredibly special because it is over 500 years old. Once Terry and Marylin had restored the main part of the house, they turned their attention to this second part of their home, which is listed. It was collapsing and needed to be restored to its original state.

The couple knew that they had to take out vast sections of the original bastle walls and rebuild them in the traditional way. They put props into the walls and used clamps to hold up the weight of the structure of the building while they painstakingly extracted the stones from beneath the props, one at a time. On one occasion, they heard the whole building creak – a very scary moment – but with patience and determination Terry and Marylin managed to re-work the stone from the original wall to make the building solid once more.

TYPES OF STONE

- **Igneous stone (e.g. granite)** This is created by volcanic fire to produce a strong, coarse material that can be polished to a shine. Granite was once widely used in the architecture of northern cities such as Aberdeen, but is more widely found in interiors today. It's the perfect material to use in kitchens as it is incredibly durable, non-porous and easy to clean.
- **Sedimentary stone (e.g. soft and hard sandstone; limestone)** This is created when weathering rocks and clay disintegrate into particles or sediment, are transported by the wind and rain, deposited to the floor of the sea, rivers and lakes and become cemented together to form stone when washed up on land or when exposed by retreating watercourses. Soft sandstone is widely used in the Cotswolds, in Oxford and in parts of Scotland, while hard sandstone was formerly used in northern towns for general building. Limestone has been used in domestic architecture as well as in some of the most famous buildings in London and the southern counties.
- **Metamorphic stone (e.g. slate and marble)** This is sedimentary stone that has undergone a change, usually caused by an exposure to heat or pressure. Many buildings in the Lake District are constructed by solid green slate, but it's most widely used for roofing today.

Wood

In my opinion, timber is the most beautiful building material there is. It's warm, natural and has a low impact on the environment if sourced from renewable stock. I love to see buildings where timber has been used. In Tudor times and the 18th century we produced absolutely beautiful timber-framed buildings. Yet since then, timber has been used mainly in the construction of agricultural buildings, as we moved on to favour steel, brick and new materials in our homes, particularly with the advent of the industrial revolution. In the 1950s and '60s we started to adopt the brutal influences of modernism, favoured concrete and quickly forgot about our crafts and traditions.

Modern timber-framed buildings are relatively new to this country – and we've only really seen them spring up in the last 20 or 30 years, while most of Scandinavia and northern

It's difficult to beat the beauty and durability of a hardwood floor. Laminate is cheap for a reason!

Europe has been using them for centuries, carrying on the principles of traditional timber-framed buildings but using modern technology to adapt their techniques and move them forward in a way that hasn't happened in Britain. We're now a small island with a huge population to house and we use environmentally unfriendly methods to do so. We had so much British oak 300–400 years ago, but we hacked down our forests and didn't have any policy for renewal. Now there are regulations in place for using oak, we should be using our very renewable, very beautiful, British oak stocks for building in this country, rather than producing concrete carbuncles. And we should be favouring local, British timber, over Brazilian, African and other hardwoods, the use of which are depleting rainforests across the globe.

The one place where it's still fashionable to see wood in modern homes is on floors. These are hardwearing, beautiful and needn't be expensive. If you can, restore recycled wood to cut costs. Visit reclamation and salvage yards to find old boards preserved from pubs and manor houses that have fallen into disrepair and been stripped. They often add character and a sense of history to a building and can be cheaper than new solid floors.

If you are buying new, avoid the laminate floors that you can pick up from most DIY stores – they're cheap for a reason. They're made from a very thin layer of hardwood laminate stuck onto a cheap pine sub-base, and finished with a lacquer. Boards like these will only last four or five years whereas good timber floors will last hundreds. If you want a cheap option that looks great, find a batch of wide, softwood boards and paint them with floor or yacht paint. I did this in my Dorset house as a way of keeping the budget down and the result is a simple, Scandinavian look (see Chapter 10).

The wonder of wood – no two pieces will ever look the same.

If you have the cash, what could be more luxurious than buying 18–20mm thick solid hardwood boards from renewable sources? I love using British oak on floors. It looks great, really lasts and gets better with age – the more it's used, polished and cleaned, the more characteristics it develops.

Wood can also be used to give a new build a wonderful warm quality, and new techniques mean that this natural material can be used in a surprisingly fast construction process. Laura and Gez's beach house in Worthing (see page 37) was a particularly successful example of this. The house was constructed out of structurally integrated panels (SIP), which are made almost like timber-stud walls. Soft wood and timber studs are faced with ply sheeting material, and the panels are pre-fabricated off site in Scotland using renewable Scottish timber. They are marked, labelled, waterproofed and treated before being delivered by lorry, in this instance, to Worthing. Once the panels had arrived, it took Gez, Laura and five joiners just a week to construct the shell of the entire house – far less time than it would have taken to build up the walls layer by layer in brick or concrete blocks. And there's always a huge advantage to getting the roof on a structure as quickly as possible to keep the building watertight.

TOP **TIPS** – SOURCING **WOOD** →

- Go for recycled wood where possible.
- Visit salvage yards to look for reclaimed wood from run-down historic buildings.
- Avoid laminate for floors.
- Favour British stock over imported sources.

Suffolk
Using a Master Craftsman

Adrian and Denise Nuttall bought a timber barn that was hundreds of years old and made out of beautiful British oak. They were keen to preserve the building's twisted, gnarled timbers, while transforming the property into a restaurant and shop. Their ambitious plan involved serving Mexican food in the restaurant and promoting the chilli plant that they would grow on their on-site chilli farm.

They found an amazing master craftsman called Geoff to help them achieve their goal. Geoff knew everything about timber – how to select the best pieces, which reclamation yards to go to and which pieces of timber would work with the building. He knew every single technique and way of crafting a building out of wood. He even made intricate joints from oak pegs by hand (rather than using glue, nuts and bolts). When Adrian and Denise had a delivery of a 400-year-old timber that they thought would be lovely to use, Geoff took one look at it and said it

George with Denise, Adrian and the kids, outside their ambitious restaurant-cum-home.

had to go back. It just wasn't right. He knew how this raw, organic material could be used and it needed to be worked so that it could blend, expand, contract and continue to move with the building over the next few hundred years. This sort of knowledge is the sign of a true craftsman.

The Nuttalls were keen to preserve the wonderful gnarled old oak timbers.

The building benefitted hugely from the skill and expertise of Geoff, the master craftsman.

Brick

Bricks have been used to create solid, attractive buildings since before Roman times. One of the things I love about really old brick buildings is that you can see all of the colours, shapes and textures that make up each individual brick. The raw ingredients of brick – clay, sand and water – were often mixed by hand and the different colours of brick stock, which would vary greatly even from Sussex to Suffolk, for example, could be attributed to the colour of the local clay of the area in which they were produced. Modern technology then intervened to do the job perfectly in the 1830s.

It was the Victorians who really mastered the art of brick production and went on to use them widely in the construction of buildings. From then on, mortar mixes became stronger, and bricks were made quickly, accurately and with fewer irregularities and transported around the country. Today, we have a wonderful variety of brick stock available with which to construct our homes but, of course, fewer producers making them by hand. This isn't usually a problem, unless you're repairing the external brickwork of an old building.

For this job, you'll want to get a good match to the original brick stock so that the old blends invisibly with the new. It's important to understand that the size of bricks have changed throughout history – metric bricks are smaller than the imperial bricks used before 1970, for example – and that there are many ways of colouring bricks both naturally, artificially and at different points in the production process. As a result, you can sometimes get a good match with new handmade bricks (machine-manufactured ones will always look too regular). In my opinion, however, if you're restoring an old building, it's always best to use old, salvaged local bricks if you can. Your local conservation officer can give you advice on the bricks used in your local area.

I would always recommend that you call in a master craftsman to help you choose the right bricks. Firstly, because you want bricks that are from the same period and made with the same clay, and secondly because you want to avoid

With old brick buildings you can really see all the different colours, shapes and sizes of brick.

Jan made sure her property was in harmony with others in the area by carefully sourcing local brick.

buying any damaged bricks or ones that aren't frost-resistant, which is not always apparent to the untrained eye. A professional will also tell you which type of mortar to use to cement your bricks together – the age of your property will determine whether or not a cement-free base of lime is needed, which is soft and has the flexibility to move and breathe with an old, delicate property. Never attempt to re-point with lime yourself. It's a skilled art and the chemicals used can be dangerous. Finally, a craftsman will be adept at matching the bond – the formation or pattern in which the brickwork is laid – to the original. Some very old brick buildings are constructed from traditional, irregular walling, similar to dry-stone, which has to be built by eye. A craftsman will know the intrinsic qualities of the material so well that they won't need gadgets and tools for the task. Most builders would struggle.

Jan in Derbyshire is a shining example of how to do a great job of replacing and restoring the exterior brickwork of an old property (see page 16). First of all, Jan really did her homework. She wanted her run-down farmhouse to take on some of the period details of the local houses in Snelston without looking contrived. She took me around the houses in the area and talked for hours about the brick detailing, taking photos so that she could recreate the bonding and the details in the chimney stacks and arches accurately. Jan had read about the history of the buildings, the architecture and the bricks and was completely passionate about it. She scoured Derbyshire for reclaimed bricks for her task and her hard work really paid off. She eventually found an old factory that had the exact same bricks as her farmhouse, did a deal with the guys who were demolishing the building and had the bricks delivered, cleaned down and chipped of debris ready for use. Finally, she employed a team of fantastic craftsman who incorporated them seamlessly to the original.

In Lincolnshire, Matt and Emma's large granary was a brick-built building in desperate need of repair (see page 21). A good 50 per cent of the work on the project was simply looking at how to restore, clean and replace the brickwork that was there. Matt used mild chemical washes to scrub the bricks down and get rid of hundreds of years of grime. (There are many harsh chemical washes on the market today that would have been too strong for the age of these bricks, so if you need to do the same on your property, be careful to choose the appropriate product.) Matt then swept out all of the old mortar with small brushes and carefully re-pointed a great deal of the building – with a huge amount of skill and patience. Finally, he sourced a match of bricks locally to patch up and replace old, unsalvageable bricks. The three stunning arches in the living room of the granary are wonderfully restored, and are a key feature of the property, showing off all of Matt's hard work.

Roofing materials

The roof of your building is one of its most important elements. Its function is to keep the elements out and the structure watertight. The roof dominates the appearance of a property and, built properly, can last hundreds of years. I'm always amazed when people skimp on roofing materials and plough their money into less fundamental parts of the build, especially in old properties. It's madness!

Choosing the right materials for your roof is crucial to how efficient it will be, how long it will last and how well it will weather. If you're renovating an old property, I'd recommend you seriously consider replacing like with like. There will have been good reasons for the roof's original construction – as a general rule, the material will have been fit for the purpose and location. Terry and Marylin's house in Hexham (see page 56) is a good example of this.

The roof of a house like Terry and Marylin's would normally have caved in years ago and

Terry and Marylin's house in Northumberland was constructed almost entirely of stone, including the roof.

been replaced by slate. This is especially true given the exposed location of their property. But the craftsmen who constructed this roof knew just the material to use (a tough local stone that could withstand the harsh environment) and were skilled at slotting each irregular-sized piece together to make the roof completely sound and watertight. There was no engineer to calculate the roof weight, no architect to dictate how big the pieces should be or how they would be attached to the roof. These guys just went ahead and crafted the buildings that architects like me aspire to create today. I thought it was wonderful that Terry and Marylin decided to re-use the original stone from their old tired roof to re-build it. This was a real labour of love. They took off the huge pieces one by one, numbered them and replaced them in the traditional way by hand. The stones were so huge against Marylin's tiny frame that she looked like she was building Stonehenge! But

the result was a beautifully preserved build that respects the history of the cottage and will survive another few hundred years.

Slate

Slate has long been valued as a building material for its waterproof, fireproof and aesthetic qualities. It's easy to split into thin sheets to create roof and floor tiles because it has two lines of breakability: cleavage and grain. One of the earliest recorded uses of slate roofing was in Wales in the 12th century, but it wasn't until the Industrial Revolution that slate really started to be used in commercial quantities, to roof the vast numbers of new houses that were being built all across the country. Slate is still quarried throughout the UK today, especially in Wales and the Lake District, but the industry is in decline, partly because there are much cheaper man-made aggregates and foreign imports available on the market.

Slate is a wonderful roofing material, but is losing out to the many cheaper, man-made options available.

I've already spelt out the reasons not to be tempted by cheap foreign building materials, but it's also important to understand why man-made substitutions will never look right on a restoration project.

Imagine the effect of plonking a modern roof constructed from man-made or aggregate tiles on an old building – it will jar horribly with the more rugged, natural materials used on the rest of the property. The roof will always look new because aggregates never weather in the way that natural materials do. Slate roofs, by contrast, are highly durable and can last hundreds of years, depending on the quality of the material used.

One of the properties that we featured on *Build A New Life* was a Pembrokeshire farmhouse that had been handed down through generations to its current owner, Anona Thomas. When Anona's brother, who was supposed to take over the farm, died, Anona made the decision to carefully convert some of the single-storey outbuildings on the farm into holiday lets and the large two-storey agricultural building into a home for her and her partner Andrew.

The roofs on all of the buildings were completely ruined but Andrew and Anona found an amazing team of Welsh builders to rebuild them in fantastic, natural, local slate. The builders began by taking off the old roof and levelling out all of the irregular walls (typical of agricultural buildings). They then stripped back the old timbers, put in new A-frame roof beams, new batons and insulation and laid the stunning new slate tiles. Tony and his team did an outstanding job and the result really was one of the best slate roofs I've ever seen.

Thatch

Thatching is thought to be the oldest roofing material there is, and is used all over the world from tropical zones to temperate climates such

Thatching is an intricate skill – always call in a specialist if you want to preserve a thatched roof.

as our own. Using thatch for roofing goes back as far as the Bronze Age in Britain. I'm always amazed when I see a craftsman creating a thatch today – literally building a shelter that will weather for a good 50 years or more from straw, reeds or whatever is found in that particular region. Today, there are approximately 100,000 thatched roofs in Britain, more than in any other European country. A number of our thatched cottages are listed, but many that aren't are also being preserved in a current 'revival'. It's fantastic to see that we're celebrating this romantic tradition of building, one that's environmentally friendly and produces some of the most well-insulated homes around. We even had an example of this on *Build A New Life*, when Adrian and Denise in Suffolk decided to re-thatch the part of their 400-year-old barn that had been covered in straw (see page 106). They paid for a fantastic thatcher to work his magic – I was so pleased that they realised they weren't able to do such a specialist job themselves and that they didn't decide to seek planning permission to use a cheaper, 'hard' option for the roof, which they could so easily have done. Despite their never-ending list of tasks, their decreasing budget and the stress of setting up a new business, they were passionate about restoring their old building sympathetically and to a high standard. The results really paid off.

Windows

Windows help to define the different styles of architecture in Britain – from the Tudor leaded lights to the wonderful Georgian sliding sash, windows reveal how buildings have evolved through time. In medieval Britain we built homes with tiny windows to keep in as much heat as possible. Leaded lights were a rudimentary way of making larger windows from smaller pieces, because we didn't have the ability to make larger glass sheets. Now that we have the technology in place to make large windows, we can use windows to let in as much light as possible to our homes. And if you're building a new life in the country or by the sea, you'll want to maximise your views.

So many times on *Build A New Life in the Country* I've walked into a room and thought – Wow! Look at that landscape! The way the windows have been placed to maximise the view is like a stunning piece of framed art.

Paul and Margaret wanted metal-framed windows but timber ones were cheaper and looked better.

TOP **TIPS** – CHOOSING **WINDOWS**

- Aim to maximise the best views from your property.
- If the windows are missing, find out what they looked like from local history sources.
- Always comply with building regulations when replacing windows.
- Make sure new windows are in sympathy with the style and period of the building.

In Worthing, for example, the huge windows on the building acted like an ever-changing canvas for the wonderful views of the sea.

If you're restoring an old building and the windows are missing from the derelict structure, find out all you can about their original form, perhaps by seeing if there are any old shots of the house you've bought in your local library. You can run the picture by your architect, to see if you can recreate the same detailing or modify the architecture in some way. But please, if you decide to do the latter, always be respectful.

Building standards today stipulate that any windows you replace or put into an old property have to be double-glazed, unless the property is a listed building, in which case you may be entitled to keep single-glazed windows to maintain the property's authentic look.

If you decide to create new openings in an old building or you're designing a new build, your choice for windows comes back to the kind of architecture you're after. In the Isle of Seil (see page 34), Margaret and Paul Drew were keen to put aluminium frames into the building, to give their corrugated iron church an art deco feel. But when they had the job priced, they realised it would have cost a fortune. Instead, they went for timber windows, and got the look they wanted by using a material that would produce a similar thin frame when painted a pale grey. This resulted in a look that was sympathetic and cost effective too. The perfect solution.

If you want to create a contemporary look through your use of windows, think carefully about how to balance the look you're aiming for with the budget that's available to you. Here are two contrasting examples from the series.

Shaun and Carol Baker bought a lovely old farm cottage in Dumfries. It was a great

Well-conceived windows can transform the view from both inside and outside.

property and I couldn't believe my eyes the day I turned up to find that they'd replaced all of the windows with white plastic UPVC. I felt that Shaun and Carol had completely ruined the beautiful old character of the building and it truly broke my heart. They believed that because the cottage was situated in an exposed part of the country, UPVC windows would keep them warm and snug as well as provide the best sound insulation. Yet they could have employed a good craftsmen to build a well-made natural window frame from timber, which would have done the job just as well and would have looked far far better. Handcrafted timber sash windows can be slightly more expensive, but the slight increase in cost will be more than compensated for by the sympathetic solution.

Sticking UPVC into an old building literally trashes its character and provides an unhealthy environment as well. All buildings need a level of background ventilation in order to get rid of smells and to allow the building to breathe. Manufacturers now put trickle vents into UPVC windows for this reason, but some people cover these up because they don't want the draught! This is the equivalent of wrapping the building up in plastic.

In addition, the amount of energy that goes into manufacturing UPVC is truly disgusting. For hundreds of years we've managed to live in buildings that have had timber windows and I've never seen a building that looks good with UPVC. They are bad for buildings, bad for the environment and I really believe that they should be banned from Britain.

In Devon, by contrast, Martin and Clare Williamson-Cary (see page 84) were lucky to employ Alan, one of the finest joiners I've ever met, for their restoration project.

Alan had his own joinery workshop, which he'd set up because he specialised in renovating old barns and believed that good joinery made old buildings sing. And he was

The window frames of Martin and Clare's property in Devon were the work of a highly skilled joiner.

absolutely right. He made beautiful timber doors, window frames and skirting boards which, once in situ, looked as if they couldn't have been anywhere else but in that building. On Clare and Martin's project, Alan made wonderful window frames out of oak by hand, which he oiled and fitted with glazing. They were stunning and worth every penny.

The result was a top-class, perfectly restored barn with the most beautiful windows.

MATERIALS CHECKLIST

- Always order in samples of any materials you intend to use and ask for three or four pieces. This is especially important for natural materials such as stone; each piece will contain variations and a single piece might not give you a true indication of the finished look.
- Remember to view your samples in the room where you intend to use the material. Light has a significant impact on how the product will look.
- There are thousands of man-made products out there. If you want to buy them for budgetary reasons, that's your choice. I would always promote the use of natural materials – the beauty of natural materials is that each piece is unique, they weather with age and are more likely to blend with an old property. If you can stretch to it, they are a much better option.
- Use local, renewable materials wherever you can.
- Beware of buying materials on the Internet unless you are able to get a true sense of what you're buying. Andrea in St Ives bought a job lot of slate online for her kitchen floor, only to find that the tiles were all uneven and impossible to lay. Her bargain became a costly mistake.
- A craftsman is as important as the materials. Don't attempt to undertake highly skilled jobs yourself. If you do mess up on critical building work, you'll simply have wasted the beautiful material you invested in.
- Don't forget to comply with building regulations and any listed building requirements, which might extend to the use of materials and how they are fitted.

CHAPTER SEVEN

Keeping It Affordable

Build A New Life follows people creating dreams that are both inspirational and achievable. The 30 or so stories that we've filmed so far are proof that it's possible to pursue a new lifestyle in the country, by the sea or in the wilds on an affordable budget. Our contributors simply aimed to build or renovate the best building they could on the finances they had. But whether they managed to fulfil the dream while sticking to budget often came down to discipline, planning and experience.

The first rule is not to let your heart rule your head. You might see a run-down old property and become mesmerised by the dream of bringing it back to life, but can you really afford to take on the responsibility of restoring it? The asking price isn't the only cost to consider. Do you know what is financially involved to make the property habitable? And have you considered all of the costs you'll incur during the project (including your living and travel costs for example)? This chapter will help you to list all the costs you're likely to come up against and so enable you to form a realistic budget. Then we'll help you put plans into place that will allow you to stick to that budget.

It sounds simplistic, but if you're new to renovation, it's easy to get caught out. If you've bought a wonderful but dilapidated building, can you afford to pay craftsmen to work on the jobs that require skilled labour? If the building's listed, remember that you'll have to use traditional methods and materials throughout your restoration, which can be more costly than working on a regular build. And do you have money set aside for 'hidden costs'? These are

You've spotted a wonderful run-down property, but can you really afford to bring it back to life?

the largely ignored, but widely experienced, tasks that crop up when work starts on site. Nearly all of the contributors from the series who set about renovating properties with history encountered these. You might find that the foundations are at fault or, as was the case in Hexham (see page 56), that there aren't any foundations at all! There might be huge cracks in the structure, or rot or asbestos in the roof, that won't reveal itself until you peel back layers of plasterboard. Drains might have collapsed or, as happened in Wales (see page 23), sewerage might need to be pumped away. Heating systems might have failed and parts of the building might even give way under the strain of new works. Worst of all, the building may suffer from structural subsidence. Until work is underway, you don't know what you'll find.

You need to do three simple things to avoid disaster – take on a project within your financial means, have a robust contingency fund put to one side for when things do go wrong, and be disciplined at each step of the build.

What you don't need to do if you're clever and can crack the above is to compromise on aiming for good quality on your materials and labour, at an affordable price. But you can only do this if you're knowledgeable about costs before you start work on site.

Research local going rates for all your tradesmen, to ensure you're getting a competitve deal.

We're often good at knowing the cost of houses that are available on the market, because we're used to buying them when they're restored and decorated. We might also be good at spotting a bargain price for a cooker or a sofa, for example. But we often don't know if £50 a square metre is a good deal for some floor timber … or if £200 a day is a reasonable rate for a roofer. So do your homework – price up the materials you've chosen since reading the previous chapter, include VAT and the cost of delivery, and so on, and find out about labour costs in the specific part of the country in which you're about to build. Then start listing every single expenditure for your project, room by room.

BUDGET BASICS

- Take on a property within your means.
- Factor in the extra cost needed to renovate a listed building.
- Have a sizeable contingency of at least 10 per cent of your total budget set aside for unforeseen problems.
- Be disciplined at every stage of the project.

Your motto from now on should be: cost, plan and negotiate. Don't fall into the trap of just using the amount of money you've set aside for your project until it runs out, as Paul and Margaret did on The Isle Of Seil. You'll find you're still in the on-site caravan when your pot of money is empty. The result is that you'll need to work in order to save and so be able to finish your build. In other words, you can't spend time on site because you're stuck in an office. There are few of us for whom this is part of the dream.

Generating a realistic budget

By now, you should have your building plans and room data sheets to give a rough idea of your design (and/or an architect's plans), an idea of the materials you are going to use and where you're going to use them. If you're not employing an architect to manage the whole job for you, this all needs to come together in a Schedule of Works. You can either appoint professionals to do this for you, or you can have a go yourself. Here's what's involved.

If you're getting the professionals in, you may want to appoint a quantity surveyor to cost the project for you. The quantity surveyor's role is to take a set of plans, a specification or drawings from an architect and price the job, giving a cost breakdown of every single element of the project, from foundations to door handles. Quantity surveyors are not cheap, but are the right professional people to price the project. For some people, who just don't want to take on this aspect of the project and are concerned that if they do so, they will be liable to make costly mistakes, a quantity surveyor is a really good option.

If you don't want to pay a quantity surveyor, the second option is to ask your architect, or builder who can project-manage the build for you, to put together some preliminary budgets. Most good builders or main contractors will

generate a broad-brush quote so you can see a general figure. They're likely to do it for free if they want to do the job for you, especially if you tell them that the job is going out to tender – i.e. that you're seeking the best value on two or more quotes (which you should be anyway). Finding three very good builders who are all available is another matter, but worth persevering with. Once you've received your quotes, depending on how the figures compare, the builder's past projects and how well you get on with them, you can negotiate on the quote you want to go with. It may be, for example, that some elements, such as the fee for joinery, are much higher on one quote than the others.

If you want to project-manage the entire renovation yourself, or be a self-builder, you'll be juggling the potential risk of making expensive mistakes with the biggest potential financial savings. You'll need to weigh up the amount of cash you'll save with the time you'll need to dedicate to the project and the

Your first decision is whether to project-manage the job yourself, or call on your architect.

COST MANAGEMENT

- List all the materials you need room by room against your set of drawings.
- Work out how much of each material you need.
- Add delivery costs.
- Add labour costs for each job, getting separate quotes for each job and hiring the trades yourself.
- Add VAT to materials and labour.
- Get written agreement on the price.

pressure it will put you under. At this stage, writing your own budget is crucial and shouldn't be complicated. See the box on page 117 for a guide to your budget basics.

You'll have to make the decisions about supply of materials, labour costs and installation yourself, although the law today states you must employ a qualified electrician to work on any electrics. At the end of this process you should be able to compile an accurate costing document (see page 124). Don't, whatever you do, forget to add VAT to materials and labour. If you don't account for VAT it will kill your cash flow. And remember to check which members of your construction team are VAT-registered when you take them on.

Finally, get the agreed price for the job in writing. The recommended way of doing this is to draw up a contract for each job. Some contractors will refuse to sign contracts for small projects, but you should insist on a simple letter of agreement that spells out the start date and all-in price (so that you don't bear the burden if it over-runs). Also include the agreed payment structure (this could be weekly, fortnightly or in three batches) and the intended duration of the

project. Don't make the same mistake as Tracy and Paul in Upwell, who failed to sign an agreement with the builders who were appointed to construct their stables. The couple paid for the whole job upfront and their builders left the site in a state halfway through the project – and were never seen again!

Finally, if you're considering doing the lot yourself, there's a tool I can really recommend to help you get your budget bang on – SPONS. This is a series of books published every couple of years with detailed information on pricing a building project. The books give guidelines on labour costs according to which part of the country you're in, how to contact suppliers, basic square metre rates for materials, and so on. They're great, so use them!

How to keep construction costs down

If you want to keep costs as low as possible, this next section will show you how. But take a deep breath, read my tips and think carefully about whether you really can take such a hands-on role. Because to get the best savings, you'll need to manage the build yourself.

If you are your own project manager, you'll have full control over the entire project and can keep costs to a minimum. When you employ a main contractor to do everything for you, you might be handing over a great deal of the stress, but you'll also be handing over a great deal of your budget. A main contractor will get all of your trades and labourers on site as and when they're needed, but will probably charge you a 10 per cent management fee on top of their rates. They'll order all of your materials, but you won't be sure if they're passing on their trade discounts to you or not, as your contractor will not be obliged to show you any receipts.

If you decide that handing over all that responsibility isn't worth the price, then there are ways of making greater savings, but you'll need to make the build your full-time job to maximise the cost-saving potential. Part-time project managers often fail.

My first tip is to generate your own Schedule of Materials. If you're a novice, set up an account at a reputable builder's merchants and negotiate a discount on the basis that you'll buy all you need from them. If you're spending, say, £50,000 on materials, you might get a reduction of up to 40 per cent on the retail price if you're a tough negotiator. Some builder's merchants offer a free service where you can supply them with your specification or drawings and they will give you a comprehensive breakdown for every single material. This can save huge amounts, particularly if it's your first project, and you don't have the experience to be able to estimate the correct amount of plasterboard, timber or paint. With a good guideline figure, you can tweak your list as the project evolves, always knowing where you are with your budget.

In addition, there will be materials that you want to source separately, such as stone, timber floors or tiles, for example. The key to getting the best product at the best price is to understand what you need, the options available, and to research both the suppliers of that product and the prices of it. Your aim is to find the best quality materials you can afford and then always try for a discount. Never be afraid to ask if someone can do something for less. You'll save a fortune if you can get a small discount on most of your materials. Remember to add VAT on any materials you buy and also installation costs if your tradesmen are VAT-registered. At 17.5 per cent, VAT is a huge increase in your costs.

Take on all of your trades yourself, make sure you get a fixed price from each tradesman and negotiate strongly on rates. This is something that really helped me keep my finances under control when I was building my home in Dorset (see Chapter 10).

You'll only pay your tradesmen for the days that you need them on site, but be warned, you need to be a very, very good manager and have a good knowledge of the building process to pull this off. This means that you'll need to know your schedule inside out – who needs to be on site when, what materials need to be ordered in advance for that job to happen, and which job follows on next. If you mess this up, you could end up paying more in the long run than if you'd paid a project manager.

Big mistakes on a build can cost thousands. For this reason alone, think carefully about your ability and confidence to do this part of the job. And consider employing a foreman to help you look after the project. You might need to pay your foreman a little more than you would your standard builder, but if you can court him as an ally, he can be your first point of call on site and keep an eye on the day-to-day running, making sure you've ordered materials in time and that the trades are all pulling their weight to keep on schedule. If you find the right person for this job, they'll be invaluable to you.

Ref	Description	£ p
0.00	Contractors to note:	
	In the case of any discrepancy between the tender drawings and the item descriptions contained in this section, the Contractor should note that the drawings shall take precedence.	
	All information indicated on the Architects drawings will be deemed to be included in the pricing submitted.	
	It should be noted that the quantities indicated in brackets are approximate and are for guidance only. No variation in price will be allowed due to any inaccuracy over the quantities stated.	
	Refer to drawing schedule for drawings used in the preparation of this pricing schedule.	
	Ground Floor	
1.00	Supply and fix oak flooring (PC supply £45/m2 - Kahrs Oak click system or similar) to ground floor including for all necessary cutting , labours and fixings laid in accordance with manufacturers instructions and recommendations. (40m2)	
2.00	Provide and apply levelling compound and sub base as required to existing concrete floor prior to laying underfloor heating (40m2)	
3.00	Provide and lay 12mm plywood tongued and grooved floor panels over underfloor heating (40m2)	
4.00	Supply and fix new mdf skirting approximately 100mm high fixed flush with face of wall with 10mm shadow gap over including for all necessary cutting , fixing and pelleting (25m)	
5.00	Paint new MDF skirting with one undercoat and two satin finishing coats of oil paint (25m)	
	First Floor	
6.00	Supply and fix oak flooring (PC supply £45/m2 - Kahrs Oak click system or similar) to first floor including for all necessary cutting , labours and fixings laid in accordance with manufacturers instructions and recommendations. (37m2)	
7.00	Provide and lay 12mm plywood tongued and grooved floor panels over underfloor heating (37m2)	
8.00	Supply and fix new mdf skirting approximately 100mm high fixed flush with face of wall with 10mm shadow gap over including for all necessary cutting , fixing and pelleting (25m)	
	To Collection £	

A typical page from a Schedule of Works. This essential document is straightforward to put together – simply state the materials you want to use and how many square metres of them you'll need.

Devon/Isle of Seil
Budget Rights and Wrongs

Clare and Martin in Devon (see page 84) were so well organised that they managed to stick to the original budget on their build, even down to the last penny. The couple had spent the best part of a year perfecting their design with an architect. When that process was complete, they sent Alan (the builder they hoped to use) the drawings, a detailed spec and a schedule of works so that he could quote for the entire job, including labour, materials, and so on in detail. Alan had come highly recommended and Clare knew that he was the person she wanted to be her main contractor, so she entered into a process of negotiation (agreeing a figure when appointing one person to give a quote rather than two or more, which is called a tender). Once they'd agreed a price and timescale for the job, they both signed a legally binding contract.

Because Clare was an accountant, she knew how crucial it was to keep a constant eye on costs at each step of the build. She and Alan had regular meetings to discuss the budget and check the project was on track, often every week. As Alan had quoted a fixed price, the only surprises could be problems beyond the contractors' control, i.e. delays caused by bad weather or by the client changing their mind about something.

Clare knew that any amendments to her original plans would cost money and so having spent a year working on the design, she stuck to her original drawings and resisted making any last-minute decisions whatsoever. She knew exactly what she wanted, was strict with herself and completely involved in her project at every stage. This sort of discipline is unusual and highly impressive.

By contrast, Margaret and Paul on the Isle of Seil (see page 34) took a completely different approach to their budget.

The barn as it was when Clare and Martin first saw it. Run-down but with potential!

The couple managed to carry out a wonderful renovation within their original budget.

They had a set amount of money with which to get the job done and took the view that when it ran out, that would be it. Paul didn't plan anything. He didn't have a project schedule, a specification or a schedule of works. He believed that doing so only led to disappointment because the nature of restoring an old building meant that jobs invariably took longer than you thought and you'd always feel that you were slipping behind as a result. They ordered materials when they needed them, worked to very few drawings and went at their own pace.

Paul and Margaret saved money on labour because they did most of the work themselves, which was great in principle, but halfway through their project, most of their money had been used up. The structure was complete but there was no heating, no plumbing and no bathroom. In other words, the property was completely uninhabitable. You could argue that Paul and Margaret never got stressed about the project because they didn't worry about a budget and deadline. Paul's mantra was: 'We don't plan – we'll only be disappointed when we don't make the deadlines.' I don't agree with this approach. I believe if you plan your building project well you will always be in control of the management process and you will reduce your stress levels as a result.

The reality of having to live in the on-site caravan while they saved to be able to complete the home that they desperately wanted to move into was hardly ideal. I admit that I admired Paul's ethic of having to work for what you wanted or go without, but I couldn't help but feel that if they'd approached the budget and schedule of the project a little differently, they might have been living in their lovely tin church much sooner.

Full-height windows made the most of the views of the Scottish landscape.

Paul and Margaret incorporated some quirky touches into their equally quirky building.

Job no: _____   Job title: _____

Cost plan / budget estimate

		Cost of element	Cost per m² gross floor area	Element shown as % of whole
Substructure		_____	_____	_____
Superstructure	Frame	_____	_____	_____
	Upper floors	_____	_____	_____
	Roof	_____	_____	_____
	Stairs	_____	_____	_____
	External cladding	_____	_____	_____
	Windows and external doors	_____	_____	_____
	Internal partitions	_____	_____	_____
	Internal doors and windows	_____	_____	_____
Internal finishes	Ceiling finishes	_____	_____	_____
	Wall finishes	_____	_____	_____
	Floor finishes	_____	_____	_____
Fittings	Furniture and fittings	_____	_____	_____
Services	Sanitary installation	_____	_____	_____
	Mechanical installation	_____	_____	_____
	Electrical installation	_____	_____	_____
	Special installations	_____	_____	_____
	Elevators and hoists	_____	_____	_____
	Builder's work	_____	_____	_____
	Builder's profit and attendance	_____	_____	_____
Building work	**Sub-total**	_____	_____	_____
Additional	Site works	_____	_____	_____
	Drainage	_____	_____	_____
	External services	_____	_____	_____
	Extra temporary works (phasing)	_____	_____	_____
	Inflation at 3%	_____	_____	_____
	Preliminaries at 5%	_____	_____	_____
Total	**Excluding VAT and contingencies**	_____	_____	_____

Set out every element clearly to ensure you have an accurate costing document that you can refer to daily

Lincolnshire
The Direct Approach

Matt Cupper made a great go of being client, site foreman and project manager for his restoration project in Lincolnshire (see page 21). Matt had only ever built a small extension on a bungalow before, so he really did an admirable job. He did a huge amount of the work himself, bought direct from suppliers, and pulled together his trades as and when he needed them. But to do so, he worked phenomenally hard and was on site every single day.

Having spent time researching the right materials for his project, Matt secured some really good deals and was always on hand to make sure the materials were delivered on time and that his order was correct. If your deliveries turn out to be wrong, and you're not around to act immediately, you'll end up paying the tradesmen who can't get on with their job that day and may lose valuable time from your schedule while you wait for another delivery. Other jobs will also remain on hold.

Matt knew from his costings that he couldn't afford to employ a main contractor and would have to do a lot of the work himself in order to save money and be able to afford the finishes and fittings he and Emma so wanted for their new home. So he taught himself about the building process and was careful to employ the different trades on site only on the days on which they were needed. He employed mates to help him out where he could and was brilliant at keeping everyone on site happy. One of his mates, a jack-of-all-trades with a lot of building experience, was assistant site foreman. This was a good move. With someone knowledgeable on site while he learnt on the job, Matt was less likely to make expensive mistakes. And as life threw

Matt had only done a small extension before – the barn would be an enormous challenge...

Matt was on site every day to manage the trades and to make sure deliveries were correct and on time.

Matt and Emma a few curveballs along the way – the arrival of a new baby and an emergency operation for Emma in hospital – this proved an invaluable contingency. By the end of the project, the couple had a beautiful home for their growing family that hadn't cost them more than they'd anticipated and had come together just at the right time. Perfect!

Value for money – finishes, fixtures, fittings and materials

If you're careful with your budget, you should never need to skimp on the fixtures, finishes, fittings and materials that you use to renovate or build your new home. But to help with your costs, there are a few simple tricks you can use to really help you to produce a finish that's both high quality and value for money.

First of all, spend money where you will see the results and design what you can yourself. If you use good building techniques and design throughout your project, you will only need to use expensive materials for decoration where the eye will be drawn to them. This can save you thousands. And by taking on the creative role yourself – thereby cutting the cost of design and manufacture – and selecting your own craftsmen and materials, you'll be surprised at how

A simple staircase of veneered plywood is given an expensive look with beautiful metalwork.

inexpensive it can be to produce something that looks absolutely right for your property.

When I bought my family home in London, I wanted a kitchen that looked expensive, without the cost. The best way for me to get value for money was to design it myself and buy the items that would be concealed – such as the carcasses of the cupboards and drawers – from a high-street outlet. Carcasses are pretty standard and I don't think it's necessary to have them hand-crafted. Instead, I spent the money on a limestone worktop and splashbacks, a fumed oak floor, good-quality appliances and on getting joiners to make some fantastic cupboard doors. If I had gone to a kitchen designer or had commissioned a craftsman to make the whole kitchen for me, it would have cost a fortune, whereas now I have a beautiful, bespoke kitchen that's perfect for the house and our lifestyle, for about a third of the price.

Gez and Laura in Worthing (see page 37) designed their own simple staircase. They had the 'strings' made by a metal worker and used a veneered plywood to create thick, minimal treads. The effect was a very expensive look – a mix of beautiful metalwork and solid stairs – but all for the price of a standard staircase. I was so pleased that this couple hadn't bought off the peg, as their staircase was appropriate for the style of the building and made for a real design feature at an affordable price.

There are so many ways of cutting costs on what you don't see, that there's not space here to cover them, but one of my favourites is with wardrobes. Go to a high-street store to buy a ready-made system – these are cheap because they are mass-produced. Then choose to have exactly what you want inside, picking the components that work best for you, but don't buy the doors – this is often where money is saved and is what will make the overall finish look cheap. Instead, get a joiner to make up some doors for you in either solid wood, or MDF which you can then paint or spray. Finally, add quality hinges for a really expensive look that will last.

My second tip for getting value for money is to keep your design simple. Personally, I think the simpler the design, the better it looks, and it will also be affordable. If you fit your product well and use good-quality materials, it will look timeless and fresh rather than the bargain it was. Ornate or over-designed products are always more expensive.

My third tip is to buy good-quality materials that look more expensive than they are. If you can afford to use natural materials throughout the build then that really is the best option, particularly if they're local (see Chapter 6 for more information on this). But if your budget doesn't allow this, you can sometimes cheat to get the look you really want. For example, there are some great ceramic tiles out there that are designed to look like very expensive stone. If you choose a slate or stone that you love, but can't afford, take a sample with you on a ceramic tile shopping trip to see if you can find a near match. I find that the best results are achieved with lovely big tiles (these tend to look more natural and expensive than the regular size) and by matching the grout to the colour of the tile to finish off your clean, expensive look.

> Buy good-quality materials that look more expensive than they are.

These big, natural-coloured ceramic floor tiles could easily pass for expensive stone.

Gez and Laura in Worthing laid simple ceramic tiles in the lower ground floor of their home – a practical solution for their kitchen/diner that opens out onto the beach. When you walk down into this social space, the floor looks as it it's been laid with expensive, stunning creamy sandstone tiles, but if you touch and feel how smooth it is, you realise it's made from ceramic tiles. They matched a cream grout to the colour of the large tiles, rather than choose white, and the overall effect is fantastic, for about a third of the cost of the real thing.

TOP **TIPS** – VALUE **FOR MONEY**

⌃ Spend money only where you will see the results.

⌃ Keep your design simple – it will always look more effective.

⌃ Buy good-quality materials that look more expensive than they are.

⌃ Don't be afraid to ask if there are products not on display in a builder's merchants.

⌃ Be nosey – chat to builders, workmen, etc. to get recommendations and contacts.

You don't need to splash out on expensive doors – well-chosen ironmongery will give a quality feel.

There are countless other ways to cheat a pricey look. A good one is with internal doors. Buying solid oak or American walnut doors to fit throughout your home is unbelievably expensive. On some of the projects I've worked on, I've saved my clients a fortune by giving them an inexpensive alternative. I get my joiners to buy standard flush doors from builder's merchants and they then bond beautiful veneers onto the standard finish at a timber workshop. A good-quality veneer will give almost the same effect as solid hardwood and you can choose any finish – such as maple – for a fraction of the price. This saving often means that you can afford to get all of the doors done at the same time. As you know, I'm not a fan of laminate floors as they don't last very long, but veneer or laminate on doors, which obviously aren't walked on everyday (!), can last a long time. Finally, finish the door with some lovely ironmongery. There's nothing better than placing your hand on a beautiful heavy handle when you enter a room, rather than something cheap and plasticky. Spending a little more on an item that's going to stay in your house for a long time, rather than on a flimsy handle that will last just a couple of years, is really worth it.

The same goes for light switches and plug sockets. A quick and easy way to make a room look more expensive is to invest in metal-plated sockets and switches. They do cost slightly more, but they will look so much better and will last a lifetime. So many times I've seen beautiful rooms let down by white MK standard light switches and sockets – they look cheap, the plastic gets marked and in time they discolour and need replacing. I also love using dimmer switches as much as possible. It's so much cheaper than having a fancy lighting designer come in or spending a fortune on lots of occasional lighting. Dimmers give variation to the light quality in the simplest way.

Finally, it sounds like commonsense, but always look around for the best materials and products at the best prices. Do your research and find who stocks what you really want for the price you want to pay. Then, when you visit the supplier on site, don't be afraid to ask if they have any other variations available. We all have different tastes and the bestselling item just might not work for you. Our Great British

restraint often prevents us from asking if there's any more or anything different available and means we miss out on a bargain. I've often found that there are ends of line, or stock that hasn't sold, not on display at merchants but which they'll sell you for a steal because no-one else seems to want it. If they don't have what you're after, merchants might be able to recommend a contact who does. Be bold – it doesn't pay to be shy. I've even driven past building sites, spotted something that I like, had a chat with the lads, asked where they got it, then before I knew it had got a number, a contact and a referral to get a discount! This is the approach to take. You could also learn a lot from Jan Grayson's efforts to source the best materials for the best price in Derbyshire (see Case Study on page 130).

Buy inexpensive cupboard carcasses and spruce them up with quality handles, worktops and splashbacks.

Derby
Making the Most of your Budget

Jan Grayson, a trained archaeologist, was passionate about restoring her historic Derbyshire home (see page 16) in a pure and respectful way, but was also on a strict budget. When choosing materials and finishing touches for her build, she found some really creative ways to make the most of her budget.

Jan wanted authentic beams in her home. When the original beams were taken out of the roof of the building, she hoped to reuse them elsewhere in the house, and her hopes were bolstered when she discovered that a caveat in the initial plans of the property had allowed the builder to do the same when he had originally built the structure. The builder had used 16th-century beams which were originally part of a battleship. The beams were rotten at both ends, but still intact. Sadly, however, Jan discovered that these beams were way too short to be reused. Determined to find longer reclaimed beams that would work,

she ended up driving hundreds of miles around the Midlands to source the right thing. Eventually, she had a tip-off from a craftsman whose friend had just passed a reclamation yard, a mere 20 minutes from her house, that had long, old beams for sale. Jan picked through them to find the most gnarled and antiquated ones and got money off by bartering. Plus she'd bought two palates of black stones for a snip at a farmers' market, which she gave to the yard owner for a small profit and deducted that from the price of the beams!

To be able to afford the expensive pink and white sandstone that would have originally come from the local quarry, Jan found a quarry on the same seam of rock and chose the largest or oddest-shaped stones to make a rockery. (The unusual shapes were the cheapest because they couldn't be cut up.) She even borrowed her workman's truck to pick up the stones while he worked, which cost her in diesel but saved her the delivery fee.

Jan sourced all of her light fittings from flea markets, where she found beautiful pieces to match the period of her property and found a local electrician who converted and installed them for an incredibly low fee. She also went to factory outlets to buy the best-quality fabric at the cheapest price so that a local lady could run up her curtains and work on her upholstery. This was a solution that was far cheaper than buying ready-mades or going straight to a department store. I admired Jan's pure approach to her project, her patience and her ingenuity. Her secret, she said, to getting the best deals was to research and then travel to find what she wanted, but always to factor in the cost of the fuel.

Jan scoured local flea markets to find pieces that were just right for her period home.

Go for the best quality materials you can, at the price you can afford.

AFFORDABILITY CHECKLIST

- Take control of the project yourself to keep costs to a minimum, but only take on the role of project manager if you are confident you can do it and can make it your full-time job.
- Negotiate with all your trades and suppliers to get the best deals. Don't let your British reserve hold you back.
- Look for the best-quality materials you can buy at the best prices, rather than compromise on quality.
- Spend the most money where you'll see it.
- Save money by designing things yourself.
- Set up an account at a builder's merchants to get a good discount on all of your basic materials.
- If you can't afford the materials you really want, look for cheaper alternatives that are still good quality and will give you a great finish.
- Be flexible and adaptable during your project, but be very strict with yourself when making decisions to avoid overspending.

PROJECT
MANAGEMENT
STAYING SANE
A NEW BUILD

LIFE ON SITE

When it comes to day-to-day life on the build , you'll need to draw on all your organisational know-how. If this doesn't come naturally, be prepared to learn on the job – and quick! The stresses of life on site will put pressure on you and your family, so I'll give you some tips in the pages that follow on how to keep everyone happy. This section ends with an example of a new-build: my home in Dorset, where we experienced many of the same highs and lows as the families featured on *Build A New Life in the Country*.

There's no doubt about it, renovating an old property or building a new home to start a new life for yourself and your family is the adventure of a lifetime. There's the excitement of new beginnings, of leaving the madness of the city for a very different lifestyle, of meeting new and different types of people, and of creating a wonderful new home from a piece of living history. It's a fantastic time. Enjoy it. But also be realistic.

It's important to remember that moving, relocating and undertaking a renovation project represents some of the most stressful things we can do in our lives, especially if on top of all these elements you also need to add in financial risk, starting a new business or finding new schools for your kids. The strains can be felt on our relationships, our health, our energy levels or our bank balance. And usually it's all of the above! But there's a lot you can do to reduce the stress that you put yourself and your family under when building a new life. This section of the book is devoted to showing you how, so that you can allow yourself to enjoy the ride.

In this section you'll learn how to set up and run your project as smoothly as possible. You'll find invaluable ideas for getting organised, and you'll learn how to create a schedule that will keep your project and your budget on track. These are the crucial aspects to managing a project, because if your schedule's under control, you can be calm and

plough through it. I'll also give you tips on how to reduce your stress and how to get the most enjoyment from the experience – from caravan life to keeping everyone happy on site at each and every stage of the build.

At the end of this section, I'll tell you all about my own self-build project in Dorset, where I created an inexpensive family home in the countryside for my family that completely transformed our lives. It will pull all of the elements you've learnt throughout the book into one detailed example, giving you some final guidance and advice before you start work on your own build. Simple!

If you've decided to project-manage your renovation yourself, you'll have to give in to the fact that once works starts on your new home, pretty much all of your time will be consumed by the build. Initially, you might feel that the reasons why you moved to the countryside have gone out of the window, as you juggle the stresses on site with those of work, relationships and childcare. But keep hold of the fact that it won't last forever and take time out to really explore your new environment with your family. The trick is to balance enjoying your new life with getting the job done. Keep focused! Remember that the work on the property will come together if you stick to your schedule, are disciplined and put in some serious graft, giving you and your family a fantastic lifestyle both during and at the end of all your hard work.

Running the Project

You've taken a lot of bold steps to get this far, and now you've reached the most critical stage of your build. How you run your project on site will pretty much determine its success. If you get this part of the process wrong, you could be left sitting on a run-down property that is incomplete and you'll have put yourself and your family at financial risk in the process. Getting things right and creating the home you want is all about sound management and good organisation. Plus you need to make sure that everything is done legally and that you comply with all of the relevant building authorities to ensure you run a safe site and produce a quality building project.

The most important thing you have to decide before you can set up your project is the role you're going to take yourself. As the client, you are the most important person in the entire process because everyone else will work to you and your requirements. So, are you going to employ a main contractor to manage the process or are you going to take on all of the responsibility yourself? To make an informed decision you need to establish exactly what you can realistically take on and how hands-on you can be. If you're still undecided, this chapter will list the tasks involved and give an idea of timing. Remember never to over-commit yourself. Once you've made your decision, either you or your main contractor will need to ensure that the following things are in place, to cover you financially, legally and in terms of insurance.

With so many people on site, are you brave enough to manage the project yourself?

Planning and consent

Your first job is to check with the Planning Department of your local council whether you need planning permission for the works you intend to carry out on your home. Planning is concerned with the look, scale, style and type of building that you hope to build or renovate. You'll need to submit design plans, elevations and sections of the building with a site plan showing how it is positioned on the land. If planning permission is required, then expect the process to take a minimum of three months from the date you submit the proposed drawings.

Once you have secured planning permission, you have a legal requirement to make sure that the council also knows that you are going to start work on the building. For this you need to apply to the Building Control Department. The Building Control officers need to ensure you construct the building in accordance with the latest regulations on fire escapes, drainage, environmental standards, lighting levels, etc. You must provide them with drawings and details telling them absolutely everything about the construction of the building, as well as the date you intend to start work on the site. Building Control officers will also inspect the works on site at regular intervals. You can only apply for building control after you have been granted planning permission. If you employ a main contractor, they will deal with this for you, but it is still your responsibility to ensure the consents are in place. Remember that both planning and building control applications require a fee to be paid to your local authority. Yet another cost you must account for.

If you fail to comply with building regulations or do not seek permission for work that requires them, you may well be forced to

PLANNING & BUILDING CONTROL

- Find out whether you require planning permission from the Planning Department of your local council.
- Make sure you have all the necessary drawings and site plans available to send with your application.
- Factor in the time to your overall project schedule that it will take to secure permission – usually about three months.
- Apply to the Building Control Department once you have planning consent in place.
- Supply them with the necessary drawings and plans, and inform them of the start date of the work.
- Remember that you will need to pay a fee, so factor this into your budget.

take down whatever you've built. This is a real waste of time and money and will result in a massive delay to your schedule. Don't even think about it!

Insurance

If you are client and project manager, and are employing trades directly, you must make sure that you have public liability insurance and that you comply with health and safety legislation. This will ensure that anyone on your site is covered against accidents, since it is you, as the owner of the site, who will be held responsible for any accidental injury. Building sites can be very dangerous places, so never underestimate the seriousness of the position you're putting yourself in by employing people to work on your property. You must take full responsibility for the site and everyone involved in the build and you must have the right paperwork to show should this be required.

If you're home is uninhabitable, you may have difficulties securing a mortgage.

You also need to make sure that you have insurance to cover your building materials and equipment on site as, unfortunately, theft is very common. At my house in Dorset, over £1,000-worth of roofing felt was stolen the night it was delivered. And it was stolen to order! If you've spent precious time and money researching and ordering your materials, and ensuring they get to site on time, it's infuriating and costly when they go missing – and doubly so when you have no cover.

If you sign up a main contractor to run the entire project, then they have effectively signed to take possession of the site in every shape and form, and they will organise their own professional insurances, health and safety standards and public liability insurance. Any accident on site then becomes their responsibility. Always ask your main contractor for copies of all of their insurances before they start work to check that they have everything in place. Remember – safety is the number one priority on a building site and a health and safety officer can stop work on site at any time if they think there is any sign of a risk.

Regardless of whether you're the project manager or not, you need to talk to your bank manager to check out your position when your home becomes a building site. For example, if you do work to gut the building and make it uninhabitable you might not be able to get a mortgage against the property to do the construction work. It's often a requirement from banks that a home must be habitable for it to have any value. If it's little more than a load of rubble then no-one can live in it and it has a much reduced value. Someone I know made this mistake recently and ended up having to borrow the money from a friend to do the work to make the property habitable again, before he was then able to get a mortgage from his bank. This was incredibly stressful.

Put your cost plan and schedule into action

While you're waiting to obtain the above paperwork, or preferably beforehand, you should have put together your cost plan and project schedule, unless you've appointed a main contractor, who may do this for you (see Chapter 7 for guidelines on budgeting and scheduling). These are the two most important documents of your build and should be reviewed every single day so that you can monitor your progress.

The table on page 140 represents a typical project schedule, showing roughly when you should be timetabling the major jobs, and which professionals and tradesmen you will need on site at each stage.

You'll be well on the road to good project management if you follow the tips in the box below too. It's not easy to be this organised, with all the other stresses you'll have on site, but a tidy project manager's office is a tidy project manager's mind. Poor management increases your stress and therefore the cost of your build.

Booking your trades

Construction is a linear process – foundations go in, brick walls are laid, the roof goes up, and so on. It's sequential and simple but if one person isn't on site on the day that you need them, or materials aren't there for your builders to work with, there is a domino effect on the entire project. In short, if you get your schedule wrong your budget will spiral and if your trades are held up the schedule is sure to slip.

Make sure you book in your trades in accordance with a schedule that you've checked time and time again and review it every day. This will only take you a few minutes and will give you peace of mind that the project is under control. Use the box on page 140 as a checklist to ensure you contract the right people for each particular job.

ORGANISING YOUR PROJECT

- Set up a number of files for different aspects of the build, e.g., Drawings, Specification, Schedule, Contractors, Suppliers, Costings, Receipts & VAT, Plumbing, Electrics, Joinery, Drainage, etc.
- Never keep files marked 'Miscellaneous'. You will lose vital paperwork in them.
- Keep every invoice from builders' merchants in dated order so you know when to find them in your expenditure file.
- Keep a spreadsheet of prices of what you spend and a description of the items, so that you know how much the project is costing at every point.

PROJECT **PROGRAMME**

	Apr	May	Jun	Jul	Aug	Sept	Oct	Nov	Dec	Jan

Demolition /strip out — 2 weeks

Substructure /foundations — 3 weeks

Repairs to walls and floors — 3 weeks

Repairs to existing roof — 5 weeks

Install new floors — 3 weeks

New internal walls — 3 weeks

Electrics 1st fix — 4 weeks

Plumbing 1st fix — 4 weeks

Install new doors and windows — 4 weeks

Plasterboard interior — 4 weeks

Skim internal walls and ceiling — 3 weeks

Install floor finishes — 3 weeks

Install kitchens and bathrooms — 4 weeks

Electrics 2nd fix — 4 weeks

Plumbing 2nd fix — 4 weeks

Tiling — 4 weeks

Decorating — 5 weeks

External works and drainage — 2 months

A typical project programme, showing how to plan all your jobs in accordance with the seasons.

If you have a well-organised site you'll be halfway there to being a good project manager.

Getting the right people for the job

It goes without saying that you should aim to employ the best trades you can for each step of the project in order to do justice to all of the plans you've designed and the materials you'll be spending your money on. There's nothing worse than buying beautiful tiles and watching as a tiler cuts them unevenly or leaves wider spaces for grouting than you wanted. It will ruin the whole effect.

Similarly, it is essential that you take on the right craftsmen for the right job. And you need to take a view on specialists. You probably won't need all of the tradespeople listed in the box on page 142, but I would advise you to use this as a checklist and cherry-pick those that are relevant to your particular project. This will

ensure that you've remembered to employ everyone you require for the job.

The work of plumbers, electricians and roofers all need signing off, so that you have the appropriate guarantees and warranties if anything goes wrong with the construction in the future. Make sure that your trades have the right credentials – your plumber, for example, must be Corgi registered and your electrician must be IET (Institution of Engineering and Technology) approved.

Don't always rely on your trades to supply your materials. In Norfolk, David made a very clever money-saving move with his scaffolding tower (see page 52). He bought all the scaffolding he needed for the project for about £5,000 and got scaffolders to erect it, with a

YOUR TEAM

➤ **Professional People** Architect, Quantity Surveyor, Independent Project Manager (you may choose to employ one to manage the main contractor on your behalf, if your budget can stretch to it), Structural Engineer.

➤ **Trades on site** Electrician, Plumber, Plasterer, Bricklayer, Joiner (on and off-site; the former will build things in, the latter will make them off-site), Roofer, Labourers (who will mix cement, concrete, carry things), Scaffolder, Tiler, Painter and Decorator.

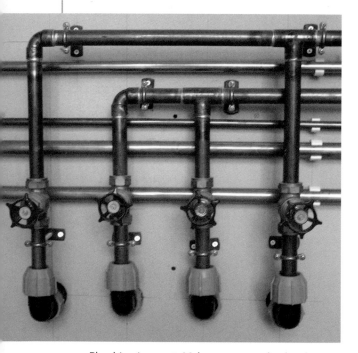

Plumbing is an art. Make sure your plumber has the appropriate credentials for the job.

view to selling it on at that amount for the end of the job. To hire the scaffolding would have cost him hundreds of pounds per week and the final bill would have been horrendous.

One of your key tradesmen will be your painter and decorator. Really good painters and decorators are worth their weight in gold. If your final finishes aren't up to scratch, all your hard work will be in vain since the end result will look shoddy. In St Ives (see page 46), Andrea was mortified when her decorating wasn't up to scratch. She'd spent so much time and money getting everything right that was unseen, only to have her team let her down with the work that was most on show.

Whichever tradespeople you book in, you'll need to ensure you have signed contracts in place for everyone. If you're employing a main contractor, and your project costs up to £100,000, you can buy a 'Minor Works Contract'. This is a form with all the basics of the contract set out for you. You and your contractor can then fill in the blanks according to what is relevant to your project. The contract will outline

Why not recoup the cost of scaffolding by selling it on afterwards, as David did in Norfolk?

> If your final finishes aren't up to scratch, all your hard work will be in vain.

a project programme and schedule and protects you from picking up the costs if the job should over-run. The Minor Works Contract only costs around £20 and could save you thousands of pounds if things go wrong on site. For larger projects, you'll need a standard JCT (Joint Contracts Tribunal) contract. Both contracts can be bought at your local RIBA (Royal Institute of British Architects) or RICS (Royal Institute of Chartered Surveyors) bookshop.

With regard to the budgetary side of contracting tradespeople, if you're project-managing the work yourself, you will need to contract as many trades as you can on fixed prices. Write to them approving the agreed price and enclose drawings with an instruction to proceed. A good project manager will then keep up good communication both on site and off, putting down plans in a letter or email to keep a record of any new decisions taken as the build evolves. This protects you and means you have a professional record of all the instructions given to the construction team during the work.

Worthing/St Ives
Project Management Rights and Wrongs

Gez and Laura's project on the Worthing seafront (see page 37) may not have come in bang on budget or on schedule, but given that they were handling all aspects of this process alone for the first time, I thought the couple did a very good job.

Gez decided that he would project-manage his new build himself. He took on the responsibility of the design decisions for the house, using a basic brief drawn up by the architect and with input from Laura. Gez became the site foreman and he and Laura became the builders, putting in the underfloor heating system and doing all the tiling, painting and decorating themselves. Gez's brother, George, was a joiner, so they employed him and other skilled trades as and when they needed them. Gez communicated clearly with his workmen, documented the process well, understood his cash flow and kept track of the schedule. Some of the jobs over-ran, due to lack of experience, and Gez and

Laura made one big mistake – they underestimated the price of the basement, which was a far more complicated and expensive job than they'd thought.

Despite the necessary overspend, however, they decided that they weren't going to compromise on the quality of the materials they wanted to use on the rest of the build. They managed to raise some extra cash and prioritised where they would spend it, which was primarily on the external timber and vast glass doors that overlooked the beach.

Gez and Laura's budget was eventually 60 per cent higher than their initial costings, which is a frightening overspend, but once the budget was blown by their basement they realised that their original figures had been unrealistic to start with. I respected the fact that they didn't want to compromise on their vision, calculated their options well and stayed in control of the whole build. Even though the project cost every single penny they had, luckily for them, the final cost was still just about within their means.

Gez and Laura saved money by doing jobs such as the tiling themselves.

The couple knew that despite going over budget, they had to make the huge glass doors a priority.

Without Andrea's expertise, Peter struggled to keep on top of the project.

The build hit serious delays because of lack of planning and poor project management.

In contrast, Peter and Andrea had a tough time managing their huge renovation project in St Ives (see page 46). The fundamental difficulty was that although Andrea was the designer, she worked in London most of the time and it was up to Peter to run the project. He'd been given total responsibility but had no idea how to cost the job, monitor the cash flow or stay on top of the schedule – and he hated it. Peter addressed problems as they occurred on site, rather than plan ahead, because he simply didn't know how to. Then Andrea would turn up, tell him the project was running days over schedule, over-budget and that what had been done had been done badly. Peter would then lose more time and money trying to put things right.

The couple should have been more realistic about what he was taking on in the first place, rather than Andrea having to step in halfway through the build and get things under control. With her experience, knowledge and aptitude for the job, it would have saved them time and money if she'd been able to oversee the whole build from the beginning. The problem with trying to turn a project around halfway through the process is that you have to claw back or borrow money to compensate for the mistakes that have already been made, or compromise elsewhere in the project. Usually, to stay on budget, the compromise is on the finishes, such as the kitchens and bathrooms. You also tend to fall out with your builders when you think they aren't doing a quality job.

To compound their difficulties, Peter and Andrea had failed to put all the correct documentation in place. If they'd done this at the beginning, and had planned their budget, cash flow and schedule meticulously, they would have been in pretty good shape. The fact that the bank turned up one day and told them they actually had £50,000 more than they thought was great news, but just showed how off track their calculations had been. If you don't know whether you're on schedule or on budget, then you don't know if you're in trouble. Project-managing is about avoiding a crisis, rather than not knowing there's one brewing.

Timing – or how to survive the process

Generally, the secret to how to survive is planning. Before you put dates into your schedule, think about how your project will fit in with the calendar year. If you attempt to work on particular parts of your build at completely the wrong time of year, the weather can make your life hell, stop work, hold up your schedule and increase your costs.

Most of the building projects that featured in *Build a New Life in the Country* lasted around a year. It follows, then, that the best time to start building is around April/May. This is a good time of year to be digging any new foundations or replacing old roofs, as most of the bad weather is behind you. You can then carry out the majority of the work that's needed to make

the building weatherproof (i.e. structural work, roofing, replacing windows and doors, external drainage, laying internal concrete floors, etc.) during decent weather and into the summer months. Ok, I admit there's never a guarantee of any kind when it comes to the weather in Britain (I've filmed in Scotland in July for the series and it felt like winter!), but overall, you can assume you have a good chance of making headway during the late spring and summer months. By the end of the summer you need to be close to having a windproof and watertight building.

When the autumn and winter weather kicks in you want to be working purely indoors … and remember this is also when the clocks go back. There is nothing more depressing or dangerous than trying to do roofing, structural

Try to ensure your building is windproof and watertight by the time the bad weather kicks in.

or other exterior works while battling against miserable weather in rapidly fading light. If you're working inside in the dry, then with the help of good builders' lights you can carry on well into the night, no matter what the conditions are like outside.

If you've spent your first Christmas in temporary accommodation or in the on-site caravan, you'll feel you're on the home straight if you get the plumbing, electrics, plasterboard, plastering and internal finishes done early in the New Year. The finishes always take a lot longer than you think but, with a big final push, you should be opening the doors to your finished house in the spring ... what a perfect time of year to be celebrating the start of your new life in your new home.

PROJECT MANAGEMENT **CHECKLIST**

- ⌃ Building sites are dangerous places. Always have the right insurances in place to protect yourself and anyone working on the site from accidental injury.
- ⌃ Check to see if the work you want to carry out requires planning permission. Allow a minimum of three months for your application to be processed from the time you submit your drawings.
- ⌃ Ensure you inform your local Building Control and Planning Department of the date that work will start on your site.
- ⌃ Remember that both planning and building control applications require a fee to be paid to your local authority. You'll need to budget for this.
- ⌃ Ensure that any work you do on site complies with standard building regulations.
- ⌃ Make sure that your trades are booked in the right order and that any materials they need for their part of the job are on site at the right time.
- ⌃ Always get signed contracts in place from everyone you employ during the project.
- ⌃ Communicate with your trades effectively. Follow up any conversations regarding changes in writing or by email.
- ⌃ Refer to your schedule daily to keep on track.

CHAPTER NINE

Enjoying the Ride

All of the contributors we filmed on *Build A New Life in the Country* described their experience of a building project in the same way – like being on a rollercoaster, where your emotions are constantly pushed up and down. On the days when everything was going well on-site, they loved it. They enjoyed the experience of creating a new home for themselves and their family and looked forward to starting their new life together. But the very next day they could experience so many problems that they'd fall into a state of depression. They might uncover a structural problem, weather could stop work, a delivery might be delayed and work might slip behind schedule. Then they'd fear they might never finish their new home. A real emotional rollercoaster.

Renovating an old property or building a home from scratch is an experience that carries so many joys and pressures. Any venture into the property market is very expensive and demands that you manage some of the largest sums of money you'll ever handle – and that money is either your hard-earned cash or a large loan. It's amazing how quickly buildings can eat up thousands of pounds and it's

Every build is stressful – it's essential that you remember to enjoy yourself as well.

incredibly stressful to realise that you've spent more than you thought or, worse still, more than you'd budgeted for. On the other hand, it's a fantastic feeling when you manage to get yourself a great bargain or wonderful materials for less than you'd anticipated.

As well as the psychological and financial ups and downs, there are also the physical ones. Contributors said that one minute they felt full of energy, enthusiasm and excitement for getting things done, but the next they were so exhausted that they couldn't think straight. One of our contributors said that at one stage he felt like a marathon runner who had hit the 20-mile mark, his legs had gone, everything had gone

> It's easy to get swept away by the dream of renovating your new home.

but he just had to keep telling himself to keep going. Some families felt the pressure of unrealistic deadlines and dreaded the prospect of spending more winter months in their caravan. Others saw the whole process as a big adventure and a few didn't give themselves any deadlines at all! Relationships come under the microscope too. It's not surprising that one minute couples were getting on brilliantly well, but fighting like cats and dogs the next.

This chapter is devoted to telling you how to make your project as enjoyable an experience as possible. If you prepare properly, take time out to manage your stress and do all you can to keep your trades and your family happy during the process, you should experience more ups than downs on your rollercoaster ride. Enjoy it!

Do your research and prepare properly

It's easy to get swept away by the dream of renovating your new home and to want to start your project as soon as possible. But before you dive in, it's crucial that you consider the most sensible plan of action for you and your family. It's important to think carefully about the timing of your move. So sit down for a serious session with your diary.

Children and schools

If you have kids, do you want to move them during term time, or would they benefit from moving in the summer holidays? Have you considered where they'll go to school and have you enquired to see if and when the school

Your kids will get bored if you're always head down with the project, so think of ways to keep them happy.

might have a place for them? In my experience, it's always best to get kids back to school and into their new routine before the disruption of the build comes along. For children, hanging around on a building site can be unsettling and boring, as Demelza found in Ireland (see page 155). Bored kids begin to hate the build and will resent the entire life change, so make them feel part of the project and keep them entertained. Don't lose sight of the fact that the reason you are building a new life in the country is to have a better quality of family life. Don't let the stresses of the build get in the way of that.

Work

There's a fair amount of research you need to do into work opportunities before you actually move. If you're thinking of looking for a job when you get to your new location, have you looked into the demand for your skills in the area you're moving to? Don't put off thinking about how you will finance your new lifestyle. You'll only regret it later. You should know whether you can actually afford your new way of life and exactly how you are going to fund it before you take on the commitments of a mortgage or project.

Remember too that if you use the money from the sale of your current home to fund your living expenses while you set up your new life in the country, that's money you can't use on your build. And don't be tempted to dip into your contingency fund to cover your living expenses. The contingency must be set aside for

FUNDING YOR MOVE

- ⌃ If you're self-employed, are you in danger of moving at your busiest time of year? Is there a natural cooling-off period that you can take advantage of, or do you already have staff to keep things ticking over while you set up in your new location.
- ⌃ If you decide to take a break, can you afford not to work, or should you be looking at a short-term employment contract somewhere near your new home?
- ⌃ If you need to sell your current home to fund your new one, can you be specific about a moving date?
- ⌃ Have you looked into where you'll live while work is in progress on your new home? Many of the people who were featured on *Build A New Life in the Country* lived on site in a caravan. This is often the cheapest option, but will it work for you? (See pages 154–156 for more on Caravan Life.)

You're in the perfect stressbusting location, so take advantage of it.

when things go wrong. And when you're renovating old buildings, something always does go wrong.

The list opposite should help you think realistically about some of the implications of the big move with regard to your work:

Day-to-day living

Think carefully about the practicalities of life in your new environment. It might sound obvious, but have you thought about transport and how you're going to get around? What about the kinds of protective or weatherproof clothing you'll need or the sort of equipment, such as a generator, that you'll need to hire if you have no electricity?

Don't take the comforts you have now for granted and expect them all to be on tap in your new home in its raw state. Instead, take

the time to find out exactly what you'll have on site and then make plans to provide your family with the basic necessities.

Manage the stress and take time out

If you're project-managing your own build and need to be constantly on site, you can soon feel swamped by the enormity of it all. It's vital that you take some time out to get a breather from the build, be with your family and start to enjoy your new life. If you're organised, you can literally plan this into your schedule.

Time off will allow you to 'recharge your batteries' (a phrase my grandparents would always use when they saw me working too hard) and to remember what is important in your life. When I worked on site I made it a rule that I never worked on Sundays. As far as

TOP **TIPS** – STRESSBUSTING

- Play in the fields with the kids.
- Take a trip to the beach on a sunny afternoon.
- Go blackberry-picking in the autumn.
- Invite your extended family or friends down to see how the work is coming along, before taking them for a long country walk and a drink in the local pub.
- De-stress alone by doing a hobby or pastime you love.

I was concerned, that was family time. This might sound inflexible, but you don't want to be out with the kids when a huge delivery of expensive materials that you want to check arrives, and you don't want to be throwing a family celebration on a critical day of the project. Your head just won't be in the right place. It's far better for everyone if you look at your Schedule of Works, pick a quiet time, or days when certain jobs are at a safe stage, make sure that everything is running to plan and then make the decision to take a reasonable amount of time off. And when you do, do things that matter!

When I worked on site I made it a rule that I never worked on Sundays.

You might feel shattered, but unless you're ill, don't waste your precious free time sleeping in the caravan. Get out and explore your new habitat. If building a new life is about spending quality time with your family in the Great Outdoors, then why wait? Use your free time to start enjoying your new life now. It will reinvigorate you, enable you to get some clarity away from the project, help you to de-stress and help your family to acclimatise to your new life together.

When their build was in full swing, Gez and Laura in Worthing felt that they never got a chance to do the sport they'd specifically moved to Worthing to pursue. I could see why, but I still think that they should have forced themselves to take time out. I really believe that an hour spent swimming, horse riding or painting can be a great tonic and make you a happier, more productive person when you're back on site to face that mountain of jobs. You just need to plan carefully when you can afford to take a break.

Sometimes, when you're stuck in a rut, you need to get away from it all in order to see a solution to a problem, get inspiration or to literally be able to carry on.

A cheap, temporary home will mean more money available for your renovation.

Caravan life

So many of the families we featured on the series lived in caravans while they renovated their new homes. Caravans are cheap to buy and cheap to run – a great solution if you want to plough all available funds into your build. If you have the room and can keep a caravan on site, you'll have the added bonus of being on hand to constantly monitor your project.

Caravan life is so often part and parcel of building a new life in the country that it's worth thinking carefully about what is involved in it. Ask yourself the questions below and do some research into the different types, sizes and prices of caravans on the market, what you can afford and what you need to be comfortable. Caravans are great in the summer because they remind you of holidays from yesteryear – but remember that you only enjoyed them so much because you spent most of your time outdoors and very little time actually in the caravan. And maybe your holiday only lasted two weeks whereas your build could last more than a year. The experiences of some of our contributors should shatter those romantic dreams of caravan life (see Case Study, opposite).

IS CARAVAN **LIFE FOR YOU?**

- Will caravan living work for the size of your family?
- Will the weather be reasonably clement at the time of year you'll be living there?
- If you have pets, where will they live?
- If you need to work from the caravan, do you know how to set up a fully wired office?
- Will the noise of heavy building work make things unbearable during office hours?

Happy Campers?

Terry and Marylin (see page 56) had to dig themselves out of a snowed-in caravan in Hexham when the winter weather turned bad. Luckily, they had Marylin's Dad's house to take refuge in close by. Aside from the weather, their caravan was so small they could hardly fit into it. To create more space they built a plastic awning to provide an area next to the caravan that they could use as a living room with a TV and a sofa in it. But being in one of the most severe and remote parts of England, as soon as the bad weather kicked in all of it was blown down the hillside. Fortunately, the caravan itself didn't move too much as both Terry and Marylin were sleeping in it. But that was the end of their plans for a separate room to relax in.

In Ireland, Chris and Rebecca (see page 62) were concerned that the caravan was too cold for their daughter Demelza to live in during the winter months. She couldn't seem to get warm, got fed up and was really worried about how Father Christmas was going to bring her presents when the caravan didn't have a chimney! Her parents decided to get one room completed and fully heated, so they could shelter inside. In the end the conditions got so bad they had to send Demelza back to Yorkshire for a few weeks to live with relatives.

A few of our contributors loved their caravans, however. Paul and Margaret moved into theirs while they renovated their tin church on the Isle of Seil (see page 34) and I've never known a couple love their caravan so much. They spoke about enjoying cosy nights in with the newspapers and a 'wee dram'. In fact, I think their build progressed slowly partly because they loved spending so much time in the caravan! Alice and Frank in Croatia (see page 67) were divided over theirs. Frank hated it, but Alice absolutely adored her little caravan and was happy to stay in there all day reading books.

Demelza was so cold in the caravan that she decamped back to Yorkshire.

The downside of caravan living – Terry and Marylin had to dig themselves out of theirs.

I really admire the families who put themselves through caravan life to fulfil their dream. If you're stressed on site and tired from work or from doing the labour yourself on your build, coming back at the end of a hard day to a caravan is not always easy. So what's the key to being happy campers?

First, be realistic about how long your build will take and assess whether it's really going to be possible for you all to live together in a small space for that length of time. Setting up camp in a caravan can seem fun at first, but living in cramped conditions for months on end (especially with kids) can be a nightmare. If you know your build project will last a year and you're starting work in the spring, think about whether you're really ready to spend the first Christmas of your new life in a caravan.

Secondly, make sure you find a caravan big enough to accommodate the whole family (and pets too).

Thirdly, try to re-create some home comforts. Life won't feel so tough on site if you do. You're going to be living in your caravan for a while and your kids are only going to think it's fun for so long. Soon the whole family will start craving a bit of comfort. One of our contributors was a lady used to the luxuries in life. She hated the caravan and was a perfect example of someone sacrificing their creature comforts to

> Make sure you have the basic things to cook the family some hearty comfort food and keep them going.

invest in a better quality of life. But just a radio, TV, some books and games, your kids' favourite blankets and toys and a few small items you know you'll miss if you put them in storage will make all the difference.

If you love cooking, make sure you have the basic things to cook the family some hearty comfort food and keep them going. I'd even recommend putting up a cheap timber garden shed close to the caravan and making it a super-functional utility room. It can house your washing machine and tumble dryer and be a fantastic drying area for all of the kids' outdoor gear. What's more, if you get all of this stuff out of the caravan you'll have a more comfortable, usable space.

TOP **TIPS** – SURVIVING **CARAVAN LIFE**

- ⌃ Think carefully about how long you'll be spending in your caravan.
- ⌃ Bring in some home comforts, such as a radio, TV, books, games and toys – even a few favourite ornaments.
- ⌃ Consider erecting a simple shed to serve as a utility room.

Keeping everyone happy

If you have a happy team on site and a happy family throughout your build, your project can be a really enjoyable experience. But this is something you need to work at. You need to consistently come up with inventive ways to keep your partner, your kids and your builders cheerful as your build takes shape. Here are some pointers to get you started.

Your kids

Get your kids involved in the build however you can. Yes, you have to be super-safe and make sure they are not exposed to anything dangerous, but the more you involve them, the more they will enjoy the project. Kids love building … remember how much you loved Lego and Meccano when you were little? Some of us liked making mud pies and getting grubby, others wanted miniature versions of our Dad's tools. A closely supervised look around the site is brilliant for a kid and they'll remember it for years … I know mine do. If your children don't know what is going on, they will soon get bored and will not understand why you are ignoring them half the time, are stressed with them and are putting them through the hell of being homeless. It's their life change as much as yours so make them feel part of the project.

Why not get their new friends round to visit the build after school – this is a great chance to help them fit in with their new mates and give the other kids the kind of fun they can't always have in a regular home. Give them barbecues on site in summer or have a party when the house is a dry, safe shell – you can light it with builders' floodlights, decorate it and make it much more fun for them than a finished home – perfect for a birthday party or Halloween. I always made sure I had a stack of scrap materials and timber off-cuts in a pile for the most enormous bonfire on Guy Fawkes night.

Life on site can be fun for your children as long as you get them as involved as you can.

Keep your kids informed of what you're doing on the project and don't lie to them. Never make false promises that their bedroom or home will be finished by a date you know you can't keep to. They aren't daft and they will only be horribly disappointed when it's not ready. Kids rarely forget when they've been lied to. If anything, pick a much later date so they will be thrilled when it's finished early. What better surprise could there be?

Above all, take time out to do the things your kids really want to do. They'll remember the effort you made with them when things get really stressful on the build.

Your partner

You have made this life-changing move 'together' as a couple. Don't forget that no matter how stressful or horrible the building process gets, there is no point in arguing over it. It's a waste of time and energy. If you get annoyed just walk out into the beautiful countryside that's on your doorstep, take a few

Even a stroll in the surroundings of your new home can give you a much-needed energy boost.

deep breaths, calm down and you'll soon remember that what you are doing is all worth it and not worth fighting about.

Take time out as a couple and as a family. Do some of the things together that you've been looking forward to and start enjoying the new life you've always wanted – country walks, local markets, village fairs, etc. It's important for your relationship to do these things now, rather than putting them off and saying you don't have time because of the build.

Lack of sleep can be a real strain on your relationship too. You are inevitably going to feel emotionally and physically drained so make sure you get as much rest as possible whenever you can. If you're doing a lot of physically demanding work on site yourself, you'll need extra sleep to recharge your batteries and keep your energy levels up. This is vital for the project, and for the precious time you have to enjoy with your family. Young children don't understand that mum and dad are just too tired for them, especially if they're told this for months on end. You won't manage to do everything and keep everyone happy, including yourself, on just a few hours' sleep a night.

Your builders

Make them enough cups of tea every day to keep them happy and treat them to a few beers each on a Friday afternoon. It's the simple things like this that keep a building team in good spirits and on side. If you make an effort, they might just work that extra bit harder to do a good job for you. A few bacon sarnies, cups of tea and pints of beer can make a huge difference to the commitment and pace on your build.

The banter and mickey-taking that occurs on site is all part of the fun, so go along with it. Believe me, some builders have got a cracking sense of humour and they have got a knack of making you laugh when things are at their worst. Wayne Sutton, the builder that Paul and Tracy employed in Upwell (see page 19), was a brilliant bloke who would have Paul absolutely in stitches even when the pressure was on. It was what kept Paul going. Enter into the spirit of things and you'll have fun.

Finally, make sure you communicate well with your team. Bad communication will make for an unhappy and unfocused bunch, who will get frustrated if you don't make decisions when you need to or keep changing your mind. Stick to that schedule, talk to them, have regular meetings, and get any decisions down on email or in writing. If everyone's clear about what they're doing, you are more likely to have happy workers.

Good communication is the key to keeping all your workers happy on site.

ENJOYING **THE RIDE**

- Consider the timing of your move carefully. Make sure it fits around your kids' school, your work, etc.
- Remember to account for the practicalities of day-to-day living.
- Make an effort to keep your kids comfortable, entertained and involved in the project.
- Take time out during the build to enjoy your new surroundings.
- De-stress by going for a country walk with your family, playing with the kids, doing sport, etc.
- If you're in a caravan, make sure it's big enough and at least has some home comforts.
- Don't miss out on sleep – your body will not forgive you.
- Make sure you spend some quality time with your partner. You're in this together and it's not worth arguing about.
- Keep your builders happy – try to have fun!
- When things get too much, remember why you're doing it and focus on your end goal.

CHAPTER TEN

The House that George Built

From the moment I climbed the Fells with my uncle Johnny in the Lake District when I was 16, I have been in love with the Great British countryside. Since that time it's been a peaceful place for me to escape to and seek some respite from city life. Building or renovating a home in the country was something I started to dream of as soon as I'd left university, got married and started a family, but I really had no fixed idea as to when I would be able to afford to do it, what kind of property I would end up building or restoring and where in the UK this imaginary place would be. Like many of the people I've been privileged to witness building a new life, I eventually found that a series of co-incidences led to my decision to build in a green corner of the British countryside.

About 25 years ago, my wife's friends the Andersons made a massive life change and moved to rural Dorset. From about 1998 we started driving down to see them once a month and found that not only did we enjoy visiting our friends, but we loved the completely different way of life that the countryside offered. The Andersons asked us why we didn't just get a base there and offered to keep their eyes open for any properties that came onto the market while we were busy with our lives in London. As I thought more about it, I started to realise that having a bolt hole in the country would be wonderful for me and my family – my wife Catri and our two young boys, Georgie and Emilio. I found myself dabbling online, looking at estate agents' sites and making enquiries to see how much it would cost to buy a wreck to renovate or a small plot of land to build on. I didn't really know what I could afford (other than not much!) and I had no fixed idea of the type of project

we should or could take on. But just as happened with many of the Great British adventurers on the series, a property suddenly popped up that made us focus our minds when out of the blue one evening we received a call from our friends, Alicia and Michael.

The simple white-rendered house with oak balcony echoed the materials of the old cottage.

Alicia had broken the habit of a lifetime and had been in the pub that lunchtime to eat with a friend. She told me that the talk at the bar had been about how a local couple were thinking of selling their small cottage and she said I should move as quickly as possible to see it. I raced down to Dorset the next morning to see the property before it went on the market. The cottage looked cute from the outside but inside it was incredibly run down. There was damp everywhere and most of the timbers in the building were rotten. However, it was set in a fantastic location, had a lovely large garden and planning permission to extend. It was just the kind of project I could see us taking on. I was hoping to put in an offer before the owners opened it up to the public but, understandably, they wanted to get the best price. The cottage went on the market for £150,000 and it attracted a lot of attention. Eventually, it went to sealed bids and we lost out to a city boy, whose offer came in £15,000 higher than ours. We were gutted.

The next day, I was teaching at The University Of Newcastle and answered a call from our estate agent. The guy from the city had pulled out and, as the next highest bidders, we were told we could still buy the cottage. It was wonderful news. We bought the property for £180,000 in 1999. Finally, our dream of a home in the country was becoming a reality.

The decision to demolish

My initial impression of the cottage was that it was tiny but had potential. The garden was wonderful and had really been cared for, but the building itself had been butchered and neglected. The original part of the property, built in the 1840s, was a one-up one-down structure that contained a living room downstairs and just one tiny bedroom upstairs. The kitchen, bathroom and conservatory had all been

On this stunning site, we felt the design of the house should be kept very simple.

added in the 1960s and '70s and hadn't been done well. The character had literally been ripped out of the building, new parts had been added over a period of time and by the time it came to us it was in a terrible state of repair. You could literally hear rats and mice scurrying and munching under the floorboards at night.

Although planning permission was in place to extend, we didn't have the money to start work on the cottage immediately. For the first two years of owning it, we used the cottage as a damp weekend getaway post while we saved our pennies and decided exactly what we wanted to do with the building.

Eventually, given that the property was in such bad condition and its original character had been destroyed, we came to the decision that we should pull it down completely and build a new house on the plot. The building as it stood just didn't have any architectural merit and I worked out that to renovate it would have cost more money than to build a brand new, damp-free property. We couldn't be sentimental about it. It made financial sense to demolish a building that wasn't worth saving and to build

THE BENEFITS **OF NEW BUILD**

∧ It can be more cost-effective to start from scratch than to save a crumbling building.

∧ You start with a blank slate in terms of design and layout and can truly create the house you want.

∧ You can make the house fit you, rather than trying to adapt the existing space to your needs.

∧ You can claim VAT back on the build.

exactly what we wanted in its place. A new-build scheme also meant that I could claw back the VAT on the project (which I couldn't have done by restoring the original structure).

It's always hard to make a decision to demolish a building with history, but if you assess the condition of a building and it doesn't warrant renovating, it simply makes sense. So we went for it.

The design of the new house

As an architect, I dreamt of creating a light, white and super-modernist house that beamed in the landscape. I also wanted to integrate some of the local, traditional building skills into the design, in the way that one of my favourite architects, Alvar Aalto, would have done. But I knew I'd never get a design that was too contemporary or cutting-edge passed by the rural planning department. The site was in such an exposed position and could be seen from miles around.

In 2002 I put in a planning application for a relatively conservative scheme – a simple structure with a pitched roof and just a few modern touches, such as an Aalto-inspired, timber-framed window that popped out of the back of the house.

I was surprised, therefore, to receive a long letter from the planning department saying that the house I had designed would be a 'blot on the English landscape', visible from 20 miles in either direction. They implied that I was wrong to have dared to design something so modern and wanted me to adjust the design to incorporate some traditional touches, to blend in with the rest of the local architecture. I could have fought their decision, but with the old cottage literally falling apart, I wanted to get on with the project, so I compromised. I couldn't have my contemporary house, but I didn't want something entirely traditional either – that just wasn't us. In the end, I settled for a simple,

I spend months getting everything right at the drawing stage.

The old cottage had so much character, but we had no choice but to replace it.

white-rendered, almost Scandinavian design with a slate roof. It was the kind of playschool drawing a kid does when you ask them to draw you a house – a square building with a door in the middle, four sash windows, a pitched roof and a chimney.

I drew every room as many ways as I could, to exhaust all of the possibilities before settling on the final design. The drawing time and thinking process doesn't cost anything but the building process costs a fortune, so I spend months getting everything right at the drawing stage. When my drawings were complete, I submitted the application for planning permission and this time the planners were happy – they thought my new design respected the style of the original 1840's rendered cottage that we were replacing. We received consent just five months later. Finally, we could get on with it.

Inside, the space is simple, contemporary and functional. I designed the downstairs as a completely open-plan space, incorporating a hallway as you walk through the front door, a living room with a fireplace on the left and a kitchen diner that overlooks the best view and

The beautiful staircase made by talented local joiners was built using a hardwood called sepilia.

opens onto the garden, on the right. Beyond the kitchen are a concealed utility room and WC. You'd never guess that this huge space lay beyond the front door.

The wide, timber staircase on the ground floor is situated at the back of the building, straight ahead from the front door, and is lit by a skylight above, which bathes the whole structure and the ground floor in light. On the first floor there's a family bathroom and three bedrooms, including the master bedroom, with a large en-suite and balcony. I purposely designed the upstairs bathrooms to be situated over the kitchen and utility room downstairs, so there would be just one exit for all the drainage and waste for the entire house, leading directly to the sceptic tank. This was a green solution that was not just efficient, but cost effective. Most homes have around three

waste pipes; building just one saved thousands of pounds.

Finally, I stole a slice of space from the family bathroom and one of the bedrooms to create a curved wall in each room which join to make a cylinder housing a staircase that leads up to a playroom for the kids in the pitch of the roof.

Now that the house is complete, some of our lovely but quite traditional neighbours walk in and ask 'when are you going to finish it?' or 'when are you going to put the walls in?' But I didn't want corridors and dead space. This design means that all of the available space can be used and none is wasted. I've squeezed storage into any available voids and created height in the master bedroom by opening the room up to the pitched roof, to add some drama.

For us, open-plan living means a great space to cook, eat, drink, relax, watch TV, play and have friends over.

Project management and progress

As the filming of *Build A New Life in the Country* was taking me all over Europe and I was also running my architect's practice and living in London, I needed to find a really good site foreman to whom I could pay a weekly wage to be on site when I couldn't be in Dorset. I was very lucky to line up John Guyatt. He'd renovated a house for my friends Michael and Alicia and had done a lot of good-quality building work in the local area. John was a craftsman in demand so I was pleased he agreed to work for me. As he lived just a few miles away, he also knew all the local suppliers and tradesmen. He was able to recommend all of the trades – Brian the plumber, Trevor, Ian and Julian the joiners, Robbie the electrician and Mike the painter. They were all brilliant. Not to mention Chris Thomas, a local drinking partner of John's who ended up doing his first labouring job on my site.

John was my hero. I depended on him and all his local knowledge to help me out and we became a strong project team – I managed it and he built it. He was fantastic. Without him the project would not have been a success.

So that I could project-manage the build remotely, I bought John a 'pay-as-you-go' mobile and taught him how to use it. We could then communicate during working hours and I could make sure he had all he needed on site. Then, every weekend, I took the 125-mile drive each way to the site and back, staying with friends or at the local B&B, often with my family in tow. This was the commitment the project needed.

Even though John worked hard and fast, I had to accept from the beginning that the build would go at a 'Dorset pace'. John had a small team so the project took a long time, but I got the quality build I wanted. I had to be patient. I wasn't working to the timeframe of a city build.

John Guyatt, our master builder and superhero, hard at work on the build.

If I had chosen to throw more men at the job or hire other trades when the recommended ones weren't available, the project would have steamed ahead but it would probably have cost more money and I would not have got the quality and standard of work I was looking for.

A job generally costs the same amount of money whether you have four guys for four months, eight guys for two months or sixteen guys for one month, *if* you manage it properly. You'll hear some people say they can't afford to get more men on-site in order to push the build along but you need to think carefully about your resources and how fast you want to get the work done. You also need to remember to limit the number of people on site at any one time so that everyone has space to work efficiently.

One of my early drawings of the simple design, showing the new house and annexe in the distance.

In terms of the pace of the project, I faced the same problems with timing as many of the contributors on the series. For example, John built up all of the block work to eaves level, ready for the facia boards to go on and the roofers to finish the rest to make the property watertight, but the roofers were busy for two weeks, so it held up the job and therefore the next stage of the build. Since this was our second home, however, the delay didn't have the same impact on our lives as if we'd been living in a caravan on site. I could have built the house in a year, but it actually took a year and a half because of these sorts of delays and the knock-on effect they inevitably had.

The build itself was a straightforward, linear process (as it always is). First of all, demolition. John came up to the site with a digger and demolished the cottage in a matter of hours, which is heartbreaking when you think how long it takes to build a house. He worked really hard to salvage a lot of materials to reuse in the new house – much of the old slate from the original roof, for example, was stacked and eventually used on the new one.

Next, John set out the plan of the house in the earth, mapping out the plot by staking pegs in the ground, making sure it was all level and square. Then he dug out the concrete foundations. Next, it was time to build the thermalight insulated block work – this keeps the cold out and the heat in, so is highly efficient. To complete the foundations and walls took about four months – with literally just John and Chris Thomas working on site.

My studio and annexe under construction, with the glass sliding doors opening out onto the garden.

We were keen to get the roof on as quickly as possible, so that we could continue the rest of the project in dry conditions. Trevor the joiner came on site to help John put in the first-floor joists, roof joists or rafters, and steel works at the same time to support the roof, which took another two months. Next, the high levels of roof insulation and the slate roof tiles went on. Then came the windows and doors, which were beautifully made in the local town by joiner Ian Fay and which made the building watertight. At last, it was time for Robbie and Brian to carry out 'first fix' electrics and 'first fix' plumbing respectively. Once this was all done, the plasterers could come in to fix plasterboard to the raw walls and skim them. When the plasterwork was dry, we started painting and decorating, adding kitchens, bathrooms, fixtures and fittings, and finally the floors.

I always recommend working from the top of the building downwards, so that you can literally drag all of the mess from the top down

One of the cheapest, simplest kitchens you could buy, but the softwood floorboards looked great.

and through the front door as the work progresses. If you have work on the ground floor steaming ahead and builders still working upstairs, things get knocked about and mess from above travels onto newly painted surfaces. If you can, always start at the furthest point and work down to the front door.

NEWBUILD – A LINEAR PROCESS

- Demolish the existing structure.
- Map out the plan of the house in the ground.
- Dig out the foundations.
- Build the walls and put in insulation.
- Build the roof, insulate and tile.
- Install doors and windows.
- Install electrics and plumbing.
- Plaster.
- Install kitchens and bathrooms, fixtures and fittings.
- Paint and decorate.
- Put in floors.

Costs

I set myself the challenge of building a modern family home in the country for just £100,000. Money was tight and everything had to be achieved on a strict budget. The main way I managed to achieve my financial target was by project-managing the build myself and employing all of the trades on fixed prices. I estimated that if I had asked a main contractor and project manager to take on the responsibility of building the house for us, employing the trades and buying all of the materials, it would have cost an extra £75,000 at least, bringing in the total build at approximately £175,000. So all the sleepless nights and weekends on site after a long week's work added up to major savings.

Another way in which I cut costs considerably was by sticking to a simple, clean design with minimum detailing and a simple palette of materials. As an architect, I'm obsessed with beautiful details, but I couldn't afford such touches on my own project. I had to make the space work as well as I could, get the feel of the building right and keep this the priority. I chose white walls throughout, the cheapest most efficient radiators you can buy, soft wood rafters, simple architraves made from 3-inch MDF and soft wood floorboards, which we painted for the upstairs rooms and varnished for the downstairs rooms.

I also used the same materials wherever appropriate; for example, the same timber for the internal staircase as the window frames and sashes and the same inexpensive white ceramic tiles in the kitchen and bathroom. I knew that the greater the variety of materials used, the more expensive it would be. Limiting the number

I love to paint everything white. It makes spaces bright and allows art and furniture to enliven rooms.

> All the sleepless nights and weekends on site ... added up to major savings.

of materials meant that I could order in bulk from the local builder's merchants, where John was well known, and was able to arrange a fantastic trade discount.

By prioritising the volume of space over the finishes and design detail, I knew we would get the basic house we really wanted. Then, if we cobbled together an extra pot of money in years to come, we could decide to replace the by then worn-out floors with expensive, renewable hardwood, for example. But to be honest it looks great and is ageing really well. I don't think I'll ever change it.

A really good-value kitchen and bathroom – both in simple white finishes – helped us to keep costs down. We resisted the temptation to fit expensive downlighters, which saved a few thousand pounds and kept rooms feeling intimate with both table and standard lamps. Inserting storage into any wasted space was an inexpensive way of creating a functional home.

I did, however, manage to create some luxurious touches within our £100,000 budget. I planned for all the bedrooms in the house to have flat ceilings. These rooms were designed simply around the bed, which was positioned to make the most of the view. But in the master bedroom I opened the ceiling up to the pitch roof and installed some white-painted soft wood rafters to look like beams. The high ceiling makes the room feel really special. People say it looks like a chapel, which I really like, and

The master bedroom with ceiling opened up to the pitched roof – a dramatic yet simple space to relax.

you'd think the exposed rafters had been there for hundreds of years. It cost a little more than a flat ceiling but the space is spectacular.

I also wanted to create a sense of luxury in the en-suite. We wanted twin sinks, a bath and a shower, which we got for a fraction of the price of a designer bathroom by installing a

We used an inexpensive white suite in the en-suite bathroom, finished off with clean, elegant fittings.

simple white suite from a high street outlet. I built in some open shelving underneath the sinks instead of buying an off-the-peg vanity unit, and fitted a great-looking mirror above, which was actually a cheap dressing mirror from a high street store turned on its side – but you would never guess. I then splashed out on my favourite Kirkstone slate on the floor and walls to make the whole scheme look and feel expensive. As a kid I spent lots of time in the Lake District and fell in love with this wonderful green slate. In Dorset it echoes the green landscape you see from the bathroom window – a great view reflected in the mirror to gaze at when you're having a long soak in the bath!

Completion

Our country home was finally completed at the end of 2003. The building work had taken a year and a half on site, but the project in total had taken four years from the day we bought the property to the day the paint was dry on the walls. Gez and Laura's new build in Worthing also took them the best part of four years from buying the land to completion. If you're embarking on an ambitious new build, this isn't a bad ballpark timeframe to keep in mind.

When we'd finished the project, we spent an extra £8,000 to add a balcony off the master bedroom. We used beautiful English oak timber for the structure and simple treated boards for the deck. We also spent an additional £25,000 over the next year on landscaping. The building work had trashed the lovely old garden and we needed to put land drainage in too. A lot of people forget to account for landscaping on top of their building costs and end up with a fantastic-looking building on unfinished grounds.

Now we've started the next phase of turning the house into the dream home we really want and have applied for planning permission to knock down the ugly, 1970's-built double garage that was next to the cottage and build an 'annexe' in its footprint, in the same style as the new house. This new building will be a single garage (for storing the kid's bikes, the lawnmower, etc.) leading onto a living room with a kitchenette downstairs, opening onto the decked area of the garden. Upstairs in the annexe will be my office/studio and hideaway – which I'm sure the boys will kick me out of as soon as they are old enough. Once this project is complete, we plan to build a self-contained TV room beyond the utility room in the main house. This will get the television out of the main lounge, so it can become a more grown-up space, while the kids will have their own large space to run around in, play and watch TV.

What I got right

I'm proud of how much house I got for my money. Even walking around it now I'm amazed. We didn't compromise on getting the house we wanted, despite our budget. The clean, white Scandinavian feel is perfect and we've brought the building to life with the things we've put in it – a few pieces of art, furniture, things the kids make, the landscape outside. The house is all about us and the architecture is a simple blank canvas.

I'm also pleased with how energy efficient I managed to make the house on the budget I had. We exceeded building regulations with our insulation, fitted an energy-efficient oil-fired boiler and installed only one central waste pipe. The vast amount of windows in the house means we can rely on natural light and so keep our electricity bills down. I recently saw a statistic which stated that if we all built new homes that exceeded building regulations in terms of insulation, we'd cut energy emissions by 30 per cent, instantly reaching government targets.

What I got wrong

Despite going a good way towards being green on my build, I would have loved to fit solar panels to my roof and a wind turbine in the garden. I couldn't afford either of these things on my budget, even though it would have cut my energy bills in the long run. I hope to make these additions in the future.

The open fireplace is the very heart of our home and an absolute must when living in the country.

Conclusion

Building a home in the country has had an amazing impact on my family life. After spending the week travelling and working hard in the city, we love to get away to the peace and tranquillity of the countryside. The kids have a wonderful garden to run around in, they get to see cows, sheep, rabbits and all sorts of wildlife they never encounter in London, while my wife and I can unwind and take things easy. It's great that we can chuck open our doors and let the kids run around and explore. We have about 25 times more space than in our London home, better views and less crime. I can literally feel my shoulders dropping when we pile out of the car and walk through the front door to start another relaxing weekend in our country home. It's fantastic! One day we will move to the country forever, but my business and TV career keep me in the city for now.

I'm hoping that now you've reached the end of this book, you can see the benefits of building a new life and will start to think if it's going to work for you. Maybe you've been inspired by Terry and Marylin's gritty determination in Hexham, Clare and Martin's ability to stay on budget in Devon or Rebecca and Chris's vision of living mortgage free in Ireland. I know I have. You might have admired David's inventive passion for his fairytale tower in Norfolk, Matt and Emma's modern renovation of a lovely old granary in Lincolnshire or Jan's attention to period detail in Derbyshire. Me too. And you may have seen how relationships have been pushed beyond their limits in Gweek, how budgets were more than stretched in the Isle of Seil and how much determination went into setting up a new business in St Ives. These stories will also have shown you that building a new life is never, ever easy. Many of the

contributors had to make far greater sacrifices and compromises than they imagined would be needed to achieve their goals. You've read about the challenges and perils of what people have been through, how difficult it can be to keep control of a project and how demanding life can be away from your usual circle of family and friends. So how has this left you feeling?

If nothing else, reading this book has given you the opportunity to sit down and reflect on your own life. Are you happy? What do you want from life over the next five, ten or twenty years? If you're thinking, 'good luck to all of those brave people out there, but doing what they've done is not for me', then that's great. At least you're clear about what you want in life and it probably means your life–work balance is about right. But what if you haven't? Will moving away from a big town or city redress the balance? Is this the right time to make that move? And if it is, do you know where you want to be and how you will fund your dream?

Be honest with yourself and take these questions seriously. Renovating or building your own house is incredibly rewarding, but it's a huge decision, a difficult process and is never a quick fix. It's also a daunting emotional journey for the whole family. Are you all ready to jump aboard that emotional rollercoaster? So many people we featured on the series have said to me that if they'd known how difficult building a new life would be, they might not have done it. Yet they've also said it was the best thing they've ever done and wish they'd done it years ago! So make sure you make the right choices for you and your family.

If this book has inspired you to change your life in any way, then it has served its purpose.

Thanks for reading.

Index

Acknowledgments
George

I'd like to thank my wife, Catri, and my two boys, Georgie and Emilio, for making my life a wonder every single day. Thank you to my mam, dad and my crazy sisters, Sam, Ava and Shirley, for always being there for me.

I'd also like to thank all of my family and friends in the North-East for their fantastic love and support even though I never venture back home enough to see them!

A big thank you to Bobby Desai and all the boys at clarke:desai for keeping our brilliant office going when I'm not there.

I have to say a big thank you to my Dorset builder, John Guyatt, who, as far as I'm concerned, is the best builder in the South-West. Thanks also to Michael and Alicia for making our Dorset dream come true.

Thank you to all of the other great builders and craftsmen that I've worked with on my houses over the years. There are too many to mention here but you all know who you are. Thanks, boys!

And I'd like to say thank you to all of the people who have been there for me during the filming of the *Build A New Life* series in particular: John Silver, Simon Bisset, Jenny Midl, Ben Frow, Walter Iuzzolino, Alex Menzies and all the directors and production staff at Shine Television who have had to put up with me over the last three years. Thank you!

Finally, thank you to Sam Scott-Jeffries, Grant Scott and my publishers, Cassell Illustrated, for all of your hard work, help and support with the production of this book.

Shine

John Villeneau and John Gilbert, Business & Legal Affairs, Shine
Samantha Scott-Jeffries, Publishing Executive and Editorial Consultant, Shine

Ben Frow, Controller of Features and Entertainment, Five
John Silver, Executive Producer, Shine
Simon Bisset, Series Producer
Jenny Midl, Series Producer
Jonathan Palmer, Producer/Director
Catherine Brindley, Producer/Director
Jonny Clothier, Producer/Director
Belinda Gregg, Producer/Director
Feisal Ali, Producer/Director
Jackie Waldock, Producer/Director
Emma Peach, Producer/Director